Faculty Development: Achieving Change Through Action Research

A Volume in:
Contemporary Perspectives Through Action
Research Across Educational Disciplines

Series Editors:
Nancy T. Nasr
Jill A. Perry

Contemporary Perspectives Through Action Research Across Educational Disciplines

Series Editors:
Nancy T. Nasr
Independent Scholar

Jill A. Perry
University of Pittsburgh

Series Book

Contemporary Perspectives Through Action Research Across Educational Disciplines:
The K-12 Classroom (2023)
Nancy T. Nasr & Jill Alexa Perry

Faculty Development: Achieving Change Through Action Research

Sara B. Ewell
Joan Giblin
Joe McNabb

INFORMATION AGE PUBLISHING, INC.
Charlotte, NC • www.infoagepub.com

Library of Congress Cataloging-In-Publication Data

The CIP data for this book can be found on the Library of Congress website (loc.gov).

Paperback: 979-8-88730-381-9
Hardcover: 979-8-88730-382-6
E-Book: 979-8-88730-383-3

Copyright © 2024 Information Age Publishing Inc.

All rights reserved. No part of this publication may be reproduced, stored in a retrieval system, or transmitted, in any form or by any means, electronic, mechanical, photocopying, microfilming, recording or otherwise, without written permission from the publisher.

Printed in the United States of America

CONTENTS

Acknowledgements vii

Introduction ix
Sara B. Ewell, Joan Giblin, and Joseph W. McNabb

1. Digital Formative Assessments in Higher Education:
   Faculty Recommendations for Overcoming Barriers to
   Effective Implementation 1
   Jacob Cragg

2. Building Relationships for Success: Exploring the Experiences
   of Students and Faculty in Postsecondary Developmental
   English Courses 15
   Nicole Brewer

3. A Digital Community of Connections for Part-time Teacher
   Educators: One Educator's Growth 31
   Jodie Donner

4. Closing the Feedback Loop on Rubrics: From Design to
   Grading and Faculty Engagement 45
   Melanie Kasparian and Mamta Saxena

5. **Enhancing Clinical Experiences Through Action Research: Teacher Educators Bridging the Gap Between Coursework and Field Experiences** 61
   Bjorg LeSueur, Tanya Pinkerton, and Andrea Weinberg

6. **Not Just a March to Tenure and Promotion: Faculty Careers at a Community College** 77
   Eric Hofmann

7. **Strategic Inquiry for Improving Learning and Teaching in an Interprofessional Education Program** 95
   Kathryn P. Bell

8. **Creating and Using a Career Development Course to Prepare Life Science Students for Career Decision Making** 111
   Serena L. Christianson and Ray R. Buss

Biographies 127

ACKNOWLEDGEMENTS

Many of the chapters in this book were authored by some of the first graduates of the redesigned Northeastern University EdD Program. The program was redesigned in 2018 to support social justice change work and we are inspired by all the work our students have done to move the needle forward on equity and justice. We would like to thank our Northeastern University colleagues who have worked tirelessly with us to make the redesigned program a reality. Without their unwavering commitment to our students, curriculum, and social justice, it would not have been possible. We would also like to recognize the work of the Carnegie Project on the Education Doctorate and Executive Director, Jill Perry, for their support and guidance over the years and recognizing Northeastern University as the 2022 EdD Program of the Year.

INTRODUCTION

Sara B. Ewell, Joan Giblin, and Joseph W. McNabb

The context of contemporary higher education, despite public perception, is dynamic and multifaceted. Trapped somewhere between a public and private good, contemporary higher education faces pressure to redress injustice, prepare the future workforce for jobs that don't yet exist, and engage in innovative research. Tuition costs spiral upwards, information access becomes more instantaneous, and new competitors proliferate as industry certifications emerge. External forces have concerned themselves with higher education since its inception in 1791; Harvard University replied to accusations from the press over its teachings.

Access, equity, purpose, and the role of higher education as a public good have been percolating for over a century, as evidenced in the Morrill Land Grant and in the establishment of HBCUs. Modern conversations and pressure began again when the GI bill put a significant crack into the walls surrounding the impenetrable Ivy Tower. Laws and funding incentives from the federal government e.g., the Higher Education Act, federal work-study programs in 1964, federal student loans in 1965, Pell grants in 1972, and Title IX in 1972 nudged higher education to widen the cracks. Previously excluded populations increasingly accessed higher education institutions. Over the past few decades, Supreme Court decisions on the role of race in admissions decisions regularly swing the pendulum back and forth on issues of equity and access. Unfortunately, as we have learned, mandating access to the physical institution does not guarantee success.

Faculty Development: Achieving Change Through Action Research, pages ix–xiii.
Copyright © 2024 by Information Age Publishing
www.infoagepub.com
All rights of reproduction in any form reserved.

Greater access to higher education laid bare deep societal and infrastructure flaws long hidden. It revealed vast differences in the K–12 system, most often along race and class lines. Higher education institutions found their new students arrived under-prepared through no fault of their own. Today, predictive analytics show that a student's zip code plays a disproportionally large role in their ability to succeed.

Higher education also serves as a battleground for societal issues. Apart from issues of access, the role of higher education in the lives of its students shifted significantly since the 1960s. Contemporary higher education walks a thin line between responsibility for students and their rights as individuals. Colleges no longer stand in locus parentis to students, but still must act enough to protect students from harm. Pressure also exists from changing social mores. Title IX continues to define and re-define, depending on political sensibilities, not only access to institutions but also funding, opportunities, and freedoms for students. The Americans with Disabilities Act not only mandated physical access to classrooms but also to the curriculum and instruction itself. Issues of free speech, affirmative action, and the right to assemble and protest also regularly affect higher education.

CHANGE IN HIGHER EDUCATION

While critics of higher education have remarked on glacially slow pace of change in higher education, it remains true that glaciers do, in fact, move. And when glaciers move, they make a profound impact on the world around them. The question for those of us in higher education, who care about the quality and purpose of higher education, is how do we change in the most responsible and ethical way possible? External forces continue to push at higher education, forcing large scale change. How do practitioners adapt, improve, and make change within their larger context?

To achieve change, to become a change agent, we need to first identify and understand the problems we are facing, both on a national level and within our local context. Collecting data, verifying assumptions, and solid analysis are all necessary to ensure the change will have the desired results. Applying a rigorous methodological approach to researching and initiating change is important to creating effective change that improves higher education in tangible ways.

While theories of change management often codify the change process into universal and generic steps, genuine change, lasting change, depends on a multitude of interdependent factors, many unique to a specific context. Change at any level in higher education includes navigating esoteric governance structures and building coalitions. All change is local and requires working with stakeholders to design and implement solutions that account for their reality and their understanding of the issue. This leads to lasting change.

ACTION RESEARCH AS A METHODOLOGY

Action research provides a framework for engaging in transformative change. It is both a methodology and a philosophy. Action research aims at helping the action researcher and their professional community identify solutions to real-life problems. Through networks and collaborative relationships, the action researcher can work with participants to find solutions that can create substantial change (Stringer & Ortiz, 2021). Action research can guide the internal work on change that higher education needs today.

The desired outcome of action research is change. To achieve change, to become a change agent, the researcher needs to identify and understand problems within their local context. Change derives from insights taken from the lived experiences of the participants. Action research honors this reality, working with participants to design and implement solutions that account for their reality, their understanding of the issue, with a goal of delivering lasting change. The products of action research are not only written reports but also plans, procedures, models and other tools that provide the basis for reformulating practices, policies, programs, and services with institutions of higher education (Stringer & Ortiz, 2021).

Action research, unlike traditional research, takes into consideration the social, cultural, and interpersonal factors that affect all human activity. Unlike traditional research, it calls attention to the fact that a study is not done, that work is not complete. Action research is cyclical, acknowledging that change is rarely quick, easy, or neat. If change were these things, higher education would be nimbly adapting to the challenges and issues that it currently faces. Unfortunately, this is not the case.

In the cycles of action research, there is a continuous process of gathering and generating information, analyzing, and interpreting that data, and acting based on that analysis. There are many approaches to action research, but each reflects the diverse ways in which observation, analysis, planning, implementation, and evaluation are described.

For example, in beginning an action research study, the researcher observes what is going on and tries to articulate what it is about the problem that needs improvement. Working with participants and stakeholders, the researcher then gathers relevant information through one or more of the major methods of data collection, e.g., interviews, focus groups, and surveys. The researcher then explores and analyzes the data. In collaboration with others, the researcher interprets and explains how or why things are as they are. The next phase involves defining a plan or course of action to address the problem based on this analysis and interpretation. Once the course of action is defined, the researcher implements the plan and evaluates the effectiveness of the actions. At the completion of this cycle, the researcher reviews again, reflects and reanalyzes, and the cycle continues. The action researcher is a reflective practitioner and an intelligent observer of actions and outcomes and acknowledges that change does not happen in one fell swoop, but from a series of often small, incremental steps that can have a long-lasting impact (Johnson & Christensen, 2020).

Action research provides a unique methodological and philosophical approach to improving practice in higher education. As external pressures continue to push higher education, this methodological approach provides a solid framework for higher education practitioners to both identify needed change and to enact that change across a broad range of issues. Within these two volumes, you will see examples of action research to impact seemingly intractable problems, such as implementing formative assessments, bridging practicums with coursework, and tenure-track success efforts at community colleges.

OVERVIEW OF CHAPTERS

All chapters employed an action research approach to impact a diverse set of problems related to faculty development and support.

First, Cragg investigated how faculty use digital formative assessments. As more courses move into online or hybrid modalities, faculty development professionals continuously seek avenues to encourage faculty to adopt best practices, yet resistance can be high. Formative assessments increase student engagement and success, specifically in online courses, yet faculty often resist their implementation. Situated in a top tier business school, Cragg explored specific barriers experienced by faculty. Addressing barriers to self-efficacy, time, risk, and other relevant factors, Cragg developed an operational model for instructional design and faculty development professionals to use and adapt when encouraging faculty adoption of best online learning practices.

The second chapter also focuses on the intersection of faculty pedagogical practices and student success, specifically in developmental English classes. As the number of students in these classes continues to soar nationwide, Brewer's work is especially relevant and timely. Brewer's work findings reveal structural, pedagogical, and relational implications for increasing connection and collaboration in pursuit of student success in developmental English courses.

Part-time faculty increasingly teach larger percentages of classes nationwide. Teacher preparation programs fall under strict guidance and regulations from state agencies. Technology integration and education is one of those guidelines, but part-time faculty can struggle to appropriate infuse technology into other classes, complicating efforts to meet state guidelines. Donner offers pathways for part-time teacher education faculty to engage in technology infusion efforts and recommends future directions.

Kasparian and Saxena undertake the challenge of transparent assessment in the fourth chapter. Transparent design through high quality rubrics can increase student success and maximize student learning. Assessment professionals must build trust with faculty in order to create and implement high quality rubric creation and implementation, but this is not a simple task. Kasparian and Saxena describe their implementation of a model that created a sense of internal ownership among faculty for assessment, raised faculty curiosity and led to collaborative efforts to enhance and use rubrics.

Field experiences provide experiential learning opportunities and bring learning to life. Our fifth chapter focused on bridging the gap between field experiences and coursework in early childhood education. LeSueur, Pinkerton and Weinberg examine university based early childhood education training programs and improving connection and collaboration between pre-service teachers, university educators, and school-based teachers. Using the cyclical AR methodology, this work led to enhanced clinical experiences for pre-service teachers and promising future practice recommendations.

The sixth chapter explores facilitating tenure track faculty success at community colleges. Newer faculty face difficult challenges, particularly in developing and deepening their scholarly identity. This identity is crucial to the promotion and tenure process. Hoffman explores these issues through a cyclical approach and provides a set of recommendations and tools to assist tenure track faculty in their journey.

Interprofessional education within the health sciences is the focus of the seventh chapter. While the benefits of interprofessional education are clearly recognized, assessment and continuous improvement processes are needed to improve teaching and learning efforts. Bell utilized a cyclical action research approach to engage multiple stakeholder groups to redesign a health sciences IPE foundational curriculum and create a comprehensive evaluation plan.

Christianson and Buss explore scaffolding and facilitating career decision-making for students engaged in life sciences curriculums. Preparing students for careers receives a great deal of attention in STEM disciplines, yet many students change from their initially preferred vocations. Christianson and Buss developed and implemented a seven module course and make a compelling argument for prioritizing career exploration and development in higher education.

The final chapter investigates supporting faculty to improve the experiences of students with disabilities in higher education. As access to higher education increased, training to support students with disabilities did not keep pace. Pinkerton and Plunkett utilized education journal mapping within the iterative AR process to support increased dialogue between faculty and students around meaningful educational experiences.

REFERENCES

Johnson, R. B., & Christensen, L. (2020). *Educational research: Quantitative, qualitative, and mixed approaches* (7th ed.). Sage Publications, Inc.

Stringer, E. T., & Aragón Ortiz, A. (2021). *Action research* (5th ed.). Sage Publications, Inc.

CHAPTER 1

DIGITAL FORMATIVE ASSESSMENTS IN HIGHER EDUCATION

Faculty Recommendations for Overcoming Barriers to Effective Implementation

Jacob Cragg

INTRODUCTION

Formative assessments are generally low-stakes assessments used to monitor student learning and provide corrective feedback with expansive benefits for both students and faculty. Ultimately, these assessments give students the opportunity to improve their skills and recognize any misunderstandings before a summative, high-stakes assessment (Deeley, 2017). Though the original primary goal of formative assessments was for students to achieve self-regulated learning, digital convergence and transformation has allowed for an evolution of that goal and a variety of assessment outputs today, while still preparing students for summative assessments (Panadero et al., 2018). These can include self-paced modules, content-based tutorial sessions, reflections, simulations, mini-quizzes, skill-building

Faculty Development: Achieving Change Through Action Research, pages 1–14.
Copyright © 2024 by Information Age Publishing
www.infoagepub.com
All rights of reproduction in any form reserved.

activities, and practice drills. Faculty can use these digital formative assessments to improve the teaching and learning experience across modalities.

Higher education faculty face specific barriers to successful implementation of digital formative assessments. Barriers to the implementation of digital formative assessments are defined as roadblocks keeping faculty from successfully adopting or revising low-stakes assessments that are delivered through an online platform with which students can evaluate their knowledge, preparedness, and skills. These barriers can be unique to institutions or faculty groups; therefore, the aim of this Action Research study was to understand and address the barriers to the implementation of digital formative assessments for faculty at a business school at a large research university in the Northeast. A variety of faculty participated in cycles of research to shed light on specific barriers to effectively using digital formative assessments across modalities and to provide recommendations for an instructional design group in creating an operational model to assist faculty in overcoming those barriers to best improve the teaching and learning experience.

BACKGROUND & CONTEXT

Faculty-implemented formative assessments can significantly impact student learning outcomes, motivations, and performance on summative assessments by providing a structure for community-based learning, feedback, monitoring, reflection, scaffolding, and self-regulation (Gikandi et al., 2011; Panadero et al., 2018; Sezen-Barrie & Kelly, 2017). The most common examples of formative assessments are tutorial-based instruction, replica practice exams, or preparation tasks for summative assessments (Cohen & Sasson, 2016; Pearce, 2018). Model traits for successful formative assessments should include early and frequent learning opportunities, low-stakes grading, simplified and stackable tasks, quick or automated marking, multiple modes of feedback, self-reflection for students, and opportunities to resubmit or complete multiple times (Meer & Chapman, 2014; Cohen & Sasson, 2016; Pearce, 2018; Sezen-Barrie & Kelly, 2017). These assessments can be instrumental in students achieving the confidence, motivation, and practice needed to excel on the summative assessments. This is especially true if students are unprepared or suffer from avoidance behaviors, negative ability beliefs, or general test anxiety (Loh, 2019; Meer & Chapman, 2014; Schrank, 2016).

Formative assessments can be digitized and put online for students to complete asynchronously, which might improve their effectiveness (Faber et al., 2017). Digital formative assessments can be built with automated features, reducing faculty load, while also delivering immediate feedback for students, by providing a positive learning experience and improved student performance (Cohen & Sasson, 2016; Faber et al., 2017; Luo et al., 2019; Maier et al., 2016). Additionally, the flexible nature of digital formative assessments also allows faculty and institutions to make the student learning experience more accessible, equitable, and inclusive.

The execution and sustainability of faculty training with academic technology must be carefully considered (Mathies & Ferland, 2017) when creating innovative plans that encompass the digital strategy for their future success. In the creation of a digital strategy, higher education should be consistently moving toward a model that guarantees resources for sustaining positive growth, developing and maintaining leadership, research, and quality of teaching at all institutional levels, and increased collaboration, interactions, and value of co-creation between stakeholders (Pucciarelli & Kaplan, 2016). Focusing on digital formative assessments and other methods of virtual or online learning may assist faculty in carrying out the academic goals of the institutional digital strategy.

The most noted faculty barriers regarding academic technology include perceived value of technical tools, lack of technology awareness, quality of assessments, time and availability to consult or design, self-efficacy, incentives, and specific institutional barriers (King & Boyatt, 2015; Kopcha, 2012; Porter & Graham, 2016; Reid, 2014, 2017; Schneckenberg, 2010). Higher education institutions must have a plan in place to invest in academic technology while also supporting faculty in overcoming these barriers. Barriers will vary from campus to campus, so it is essential to focus on the many barriers already in the literature, while also probing faculty to share their own experiences and play an integral role in identifying and overcoming barriers at specific institutions. Increased academic technology usage has put tension on faculty, changing the balance of focus between teaching and other responsibilities, such as research (Polly et al., 2021). A plan to mitigate and minimize these barriers to implementation is necessary for institutional success, knowing that positive technology experiences for faculty can lead to higher levels of self-efficacy with academic technology and may lead to increased adoption or revision rates of digital formative assessments (Buchanan et al., 2013; Reid, 2014, 2017).

To successfully carry out the institutional strategy and assist stakeholders in overcoming barriers, higher education institutions will look to faculty development, instructional design services, and academic technology support. Emerging pedagogical trends, combined with new online, virtual, and hybrid course modalities, are going to provide institutions with more justification for investing in academic technology moving forward (Beatty, 2019; Darby & Lang, 2019). Additionally, there are new methodologies and technologies for faculty to learn for these modalities, such as Universal Design for Learning (UDL), virtual classes, lecture-capture, accessibility reporting, content authoring software, and other third-party integrations within learning management systems (Capp, 2017; Lapitan et al., 2021; McKenzie, 2018). With faculty serving as the content experts, academic technologists, instructional designers, and other pedagogical experts will be essential in assisting faculty to navigate many of the barriers that will come from this transition in course development and the learner experience (Reid, 2014, 2017).

This study is situated in the gap in the literature regarding specific recommendations from faculty to technology groups in overcoming the specific barriers. The literature does suggest that designers, technologists, and other pedagogical staff should begin by forming an extensive relationship and building positive rapport with faculty and other university stakeholders. Some key elements of that relationship include understanding the roles of the faculty and staff, mutual trust, customized support, and buy-in from the faculty (Richardson et al., 2018). A recent shift in roles due to the COVID-19 pandemic required institutional staff to gather, organize, and distribute resources, design, and deliver new faculty course development workshops, provide increased technical support, and advocate for student learning and for their own positions (Xie et al., 2021). Robust training programs should be implemented to transition faculty from traditional teaching to new modalities, which will require an extensive reliance on the building of relationships within the university community (Xie et al., 2021). An institution's digital strategy should include plans for additional funding and staffing academic technology groups (Darby & Lang, 2019; Mathies & Ferland, 2017; Melear, 2017), as well as the continued investment in classroom technology, which has been heightened due to the COVID-19 pandemic. Staff should develop and model learner-centered and pedagogically supported faculty development, implementing principles of Universal Design for Learning (UDL), design theory, project-based learning, and professional learning communities (PLCs) (Brown & Green, 2017; Capp, 2017; Gilboy et al., 2015).

METHODS

A business school at a large research university in the Northeast was selected as the site for this study. At this business school an instructional design group works with faculty and staff to deliver professional development, instructional design services, and academic technology support that improve the teaching and learning experience. Taking the Action Research methodology from theory to practice in this study allowed the design group to use data collected through faculty experiences and recommendations to address the specific needs of the participants and other institutional stakeholders (Stringer, 2014).

Seven faculty at the business school agreed to participate in Cycle 1 of this study. A variety of full-time and part-time faculty were chosen to participate based on the issues that concerned them regarding development, services, and support provided by the school. In addition, these faculty had previous experience working with the design group and were aware of some of the training and resources available to them. Participants also represented a mix of traditional, hybrid, and online delivery methods, while faculty who had not previously worked with the design group were excluded from this cycle of research. Initially, faculty participated in a semi-structured interview lasting from 20–30 minutes with a protocol that focused on the unique experiences of faculty with academic technology and digital formative assessments. The goal of Cycle 1 was to gather data from faculty about the barriers and benefits of adopting or revising digital formative assessments across modalities at the business school, and then gather specific recommendations for the design group on development, services, and support that would increase faculty adoption and revision. Data was collected, reviewed, unitized, and categorized before being organized and disseminated (Stringer, 2014).

In Cycle 2, six participants from Cycle 1 were joined by six additional full-time and part-time faculty, for a total of 12 participants. This allowed for faculty not responsible for the initial recommendations to participate in the evaluation of the model. The participation criteria from Cycle 1 was continued in Cycle 2, with the addition of purposefully selecting additional faculty to have participant representation across all academic departments, as well as other undergraduate and graduate programs. Based on Cycle 1 data, a new operational model based on faculty recommendations was created. The recommended action steps in this model included faculty showcase events, an onboarding course, and new communication, instructional design, and academic technology support strategies. Cycle 2 provided an opportunity to enrich the analysis further by adding faculty participants and providing specific evidence of participant engagement and experience with this operational model and the embedded action steps. Faculty participated in five short semi-structured interviews, evaluating each action step individually. The overall effectiveness and trustworthiness of this study was assessed by analyzing qualitative data throughout, such as analytic memos from participant member check-ins and semi-structured interview transcripts as well as analysis of the design group's data. Occasionally, some of this data was quantified based on faculty responses and information gathered.

CYCLE 1 RESULTS

In Cycle 1 data analysis, three major themes emerged: faculty motivations for using digital formative assessments, faculty barriers to adopting or revising digital formative assessments, faculty recommendations for professional development, instructional design services, and academic technology support.

Faculty Motivations for Using Digital Formative Assessments

Types of digital formative assessments that business faculty were currently using or had used in the past included simulations, reflections, quizzes, journals, polls, discussions, and modules. Most faculty indicated they were highly motivated to use digital formative assessments by the need to incorporate relevant delivery, material, and content as well as the desire to improve on their teaching and increase student engagement and teaching evaluation scores. Many felt that digital formative assessments improved their teaching, positively affected the students' perspectives of the class, were convenient and necessary in online or hybrid courses, and could possibly improve the school's rankings amongst peer institutions. Since both the benefits and motivations for faculty to use formative assessments in their courses are well established in the literature, that theme was not the focus of this study (Maier et al., 2016; Meer & Chapman, 2014; Pearce, 2018; Petrovic et al., 2017; Schrank, 2016; Sezen-Barrie & Kelly, 2017).

Faculty Barriers for Adopting or Revising Digital Formative Assessments

Faculty interviews revealed barriers to successfully implementing digital formative assessments including a steep learning curve, self-efficacy concerns, lack of time and availability, and awareness of development, services, and support. In reviewing the literature, faculty barriers to effective implementation of academic technology include perceived value of tools, lack of faculty awareness of technology, quality of assessments, self-efficacy, time and availability to consult or design, technical skills, faculty incentives, and other institutional barriers (King & Boyatt, 2015; Porter & Graham, 2016; Reid, 2014, 2017). The Cycle 1 findings reinforced these general barriers to academic technology found in the literature and slightly expanded the list in relation to digital formative assessments, such as the addition of the fear or risk of using academic technology barrier.

Faculty Recommendations for Development, Services, and Support

Recommendations from faculty for overcoming these barriers included the ideas of faculty showcase sessions, onboarding new faculty, better promotion of the design group's services and events, customized in-house design, and tailored instruction and support. Though technology groups make informed and evidence-based decisions on software or strategy integration, the Cycle 1 data analysis of this study allows for the researcher to analyze and implement faculty recommendations in creating a model of faculty development, instructional design services, and academic technology support in overcoming the barriers to effective implementation of digital formative assessments. Recommendations and feedback gathered in Cycle 1 informed the action steps created for Cycle 2.

OVERVIEW OF CYCLE 2

An operational model of faculty development, services, and support was created to specifically put Cycle 1 faculty recommendations into action. This model included five recommended action steps: a faculty showcase event on digital formative assessments, an onboarding repository with self-paced modules, a new communication strategy with a new website, automated email and event systems, and Microsoft Teams, more customized in-house design opportunities for faculty, and customized academic technology support. Over the course of the Fall 2020 semester, participating faculty engaged in all five action steps with the design group. The objectives of these action steps were to reestablish and uncover new faculty barriers and to solidify the operational model for faculty development, instructional design services, and academic technology support that assisted faculty in overcoming barriers to effective implementation of digital formative assessments.

Faculty participants began engaging in the action steps by attending (synchronously or asynchronously) at least one of the design group's faculty showcase events. Based on Cycle 1 data analysis, faculty recommended that events should feature examples of digital formative assessments from their colleagues. Then, participating faculty were enrolled in a self-paced onboarding course in Canvas and asked to explore the resources, a request from new and part-time faculty in Cycle 1. Specifically addressing the barrier of awareness, the design group created a new communication strategy which including a new webpage, email service, and utilization of Microsoft Teams. Participants engaged with all three communication activities and data was gathered on their preferences and the effectiveness of the strategy. Next, faculty engaged with design staff to address their personal assessment design needs across modalities. And lastly, the design group created a new system of academic technology support by streamlining appointment scheduling with staff. New full-time and part-time staff members were hired to meet the increased demands of faculty support and were available to answer urgent questions or provide just-in-time consultations for all academic technology, including assessment delivery assistance within the business context.

Cycle 2 Results

The action steps were evaluated on whether faculty barriers were reduced or eliminated and how likely faculty were to adopt or revise digital formative assessments having engaged in the action steps. Faculty participated in regular member check-ins throughout the Fall 2020 and Spring 2021 semesters. After engaging with all the action steps, faculty participated in five semi-structured interviews, with each interview discussing and evaluating a different action step. Data gathered demonstrated that all five action steps were effective in reducing or eliminating faculty barriers and that faculty were more likely to adopt or revise digital formative assessments in the future.

An ongoing theme in both Cycles 1 and 2, faculty identified many barriers across all five action steps, including skills and self-efficacy, fear/risk of academic technology, awareness of resources, and time and availability. Additional information gathered on faculty barriers in Cycle 2 specifically, reinforced the success of this objective by further informing the design group on new barriers, such as information overload, and additional faculty needs regarding the effective implementation of digital formative assessments.

Each of the five action steps used to create this model demonstrated to be 100% successful in either reducing or eliminating the faculty barriers uncovered in Cycles 1 and 2. In addition, after engaging with the Cycle 2 action steps, 100% of participating faculty found that at least three of the five changes would help improve the effectiveness of the digital formative assessments they implemented in their courses, with 83% of faculty saying that all five were effective in accomplishing that goal. With the new faculty development, instructional design services, and academic technology support model, the design group has built a better system for digital formative assessments. Through this model, the design group has also improved communication and rapport with stakeholders and the user experience for both faculty and students. Overall, these action steps were successful in effecting meaningful change at the business school. Detailed results of the study in relation to the literature, context, and implications for practice can be found in the following discussion section which examines five specific findings, one for each action step taken in Cycle 2.

DISCUSSION

Showcase Events Provided Insight and Inspiration for Faculty

All faculty participants found the faculty showcase events to be effective in reducing or eliminating barriers with the majority of participants responding that they were more likely to adopt or revise digital formative assessments in the future. This finding is first situated within the literature that details the importance of the learner-centered professional development model, especially when transitioning faculty from a traditional to an online or hybrid course modality (Darby & Lang, 2019; Yee, 2015; Xie et al., 2021). This finding expanded the literature by providing an additional actionable item for academic technology or instructional design groups that fits well within the cited learner-centered model.

The faculty showcase events also confirmed the reduction or elimination of barriers, such as awareness and time uncovered in the literature (King & Boyatt, 2015; Kopcha, 2012; Porter & Graham, 2016; Reid, 2014, 2017; Schneckenberg, 2010). Faculty showcase events can be applied to all teaching methodologies and tools for teaching and learning and not reserved just for digital formative assessments. These recorded events can be the cornerstone of virtual PLCs hosted on Canvas, allowing faculty to engage with them asynchronously at their convenience or when appropriate. By doing this, the business school can make professional development sessions more accessible, engaging, and robust for faculty and staff. This finding is an example of the faculty development piece of the operational model along with the second finding, the faculty onboarding course.

Onboarding Course Filled Faculty Learning Gap

All faculty participants found the faculty onboarding course to be effective in reducing or eliminating barriers, with most participants responding that they were more likely to adopt or revise digital formative assessments in the future. Like the faculty showcase events, the onboarding course is situated within and is supported by the literature on the learner-centered model for faculty development (Darby & Lang, 2019; Yee, 2015; Xie et al., 2021). This finding provides faculty with an asynchronous option for increasing their knowledge and improving their skills with academic technology and digital formative assessments. It is also a representation of what Xie et al. (2021) mention regarding the shifting roles for technologists and designers due to the COVID-19 pandemic, transitioning to make professional development more accessible online.

The onboarding course focused more on faculty's self-efficacy concerns, further supporting additional literature, than the faculty showcase events (Buchanan et al., 2013; Reid, 2017; Wingo et al., 2017). In engaging with the onboarding course, faculty also reported a new barrier called information overload. Most likely due to the COVID-19 pandemic and change from traditional to emergency remote learning, faculty reported that there was a significant uptick in information coming from institution officials. By having the onboarding course as an option for new or interested faculty, participants responded that it helped cut through the noise by having a lot of information in a single space.

Communication Strategy Successfully Combatted Barriers

All faculty participants found the new communication strategy to be effective in reducing or eliminating barriers and reported that they were more likely to attend an event on digital formative assessments in the future. The design group can better manage costs and increase attendance by using an effective communication strategy and focusing on the needs of faculty and addressing specific learning outcomes and objectives within the digital context (Ghemawat, 2017; Mathies & Ferland, 2017). Having an effective communication strategy, faculty are more informed about the group's strategies, events, and services, leading to increased collaboration and co-creation between internal stakeholders (Pucciarelli & Kaplan, 2016). To effectively communicate with internal stakeholders, institutions must have a sense of where the successes and failures lie in regard to the digital strategy (Mathies & Ferland, 2017).

Barriers uncovered in this finding were mostly focused on the awareness and the information overload barriers, further confirming the literature on the awareness barrier and expanding the literature with the information overload barrier (King & Boyatt, 2015; Kopcha, 2012; Porter & Graham, 2016; Reid, 2014, 2017; Schneckenberg, 2010). Additionally, this finding included email data that confirmed that the new email had higher open rates and gained more registrations than its previous counterpart. This information fits within the consideration for faculty's future technology needs as a necessary part of the digital strategy (Beatty, 2019; Mathies & Ferland, 2017). Institutions and organizations should select the appropriate tools and methods of delivery after gathering feedback through appropriate piloting (Beatty, 2019; Mathies & Ferland, 2017). Feedback from faculty regarding the new communication strategy is essential for how information on development, services, and support are delivered in the future.

Instructional Design Strategy Improved Faculty Confidence

All faculty participants found the instructional design strategy to be effective in reducing or eliminating barriers and that they were more likely to adopt or revise digital formative assessments in the future. This finding spoke to the desire for faculty to create formative assessments to monitor and support student learning throughout an online, hybrid, or traditional course (Gikandi et al., 2011; Sezen-Barrie & Kelly, 2017). Faculty appreciated the assistance in designing the tutorial-based learning opportunities, better preparing students for summative assessments (Pearce, 2018). Having engaged in the action steps, participating faculty reported that the student experience was improved, confirming the literature regarding the benefits for students (Faber et al., 2017; Loh, 2019; McCarthy, 2017; Meer & Chapman, 2014; Pearce, 2018; Schrank, 2016). Specifically, faculty addressed the positive learning outcomes as a benefit for students, as well as a motivation for faculty (McCarthy, 2017; Porter & Graham, 2016). By digitizing these learning opportunities, faculty can approach the learning experience in a more flexible fashion, likely increasing engagement and improving student performance based on the literature (Cohen & Sasson, 2016; Faber et al., 2017; Luo et al., 2019). The popularity of digital formative assessments in online and blended courses was also mentioned by participating faculty (Heilporn & Lakhal, 2021).

Again, time was a barrier overcome by faculty in this action step (King & Boyatt, 2015; Kopcha, 2012; Porter & Graham, 2016; Reid, 2014; Reid, 2017; Schneckenberg, 2010), but this finding expanded upon the literature to include the time and availability of the design group staff. This finding provides more justification for using digital formative assessments at the business school, as well as the strategy for staff assisting faculty in this endeavor. In Cycle 1, faculty asked for more customized in-house design opportunities. By employing more dedicated design staff, the group was able to invest in faculty's recommendations, rather than exclusively relying on publisher-created content. This finding allows faculty ideas to come to light by removing the barriers and allowing for easy access of collaborative resources. Additionally, this finding shows the design group's ability to efficiently create and deliver customized assessments in a cost- and resource-effective manner. With the group creating more customized digital formative assessments for faculty, additional academic technology support was necessary in the model to reduce barriers, maintain rapport, and increase faculty satisfaction.

Academic Technology Support Strategy Increased Staff Accessibility

All faculty participants found the academic technology support strategy to be effective in reducing or eliminating barriers and that they were more likely to adopt or revise digital formative assessments in the future. This finding confirms that customized technical support is needed to best sustain institutional and faculty motivations for using academic technology in the classroom (Buchanan et al., 2013). The support finding is first situated within the institutional need to create a digital strategy that is focusing on evolving needs of faculty and students, as well as improving teaching and collaboration between internal stakeholders (Mathies & Ferland, 2017; Pucciarelli & Kaplan, 2016). The literature provides a game plan for technologists and designers by stating the importance of trust and rapport building to achieve buy-in for faculty, which is exactly how this Action Research study was accomplished (Richardson et al., 2018). Xie et al. (2021) also contend that due to the shift in roles caused by the COVID-19 pandemic, technologists and designers must provide increased technical support to keep up with demand. This finding supports that literature in that the design group completed more support tickets during 2020 than any other year in their history.

Time, fear/risk, and self-efficacy were all barriers overcome by faculty in this final piece of the operational model (Buchanan et al., 2013; King & Boyatt, 2015; Kopcha, 2012; Porter & Graham, 2016; Reid, 2014, 2017; Schneckenberg, 2010; Wingo et al., 2017). With additional staff dedicated to providing customized academic technology support for faculty creating digital formative assessments, the design group can use this finding to improve support strategy across all operations. The academic technology support strategy finding confirms that the design group has made the appropriate changes to successfully sustain the model of faculty development, instructional design services, and academic technology support to positively influence faculty's usage of digital formative assessments in the classroom.

FUTURE RESEARCH

The operational model detailed in this study may act as a blueprint for other instructional design or academic technology teams to effect change based on the specific needs of their own faculty and stakeholders. However, some of the specific faculty barriers to successful implementation of digital formative assessments mentioned in this study may be unique to the individual faculty, academic departments, or institution presented. Additionally, with this study being performed at a site with dedicated resources for academic technology and instructional design, limitations exist when applying this study to institutions with fewer available resources or a more centralized approach to faculty development, design services, and technology support.

The design group will continue cyclical Action Research to uncover and address new barriers as they arise and continue the forward momentum that was brought about because of this research. Beyond this study, the design group will focus on its inclusive design efforts, partnering with new internal and external stakeholders to recognize and empower a variety of voices and perspectives. In doing so, future research on digital formative assessments will include student recommendations for faculty and staff. The model for development, services, and support will be applied across other operations within the design group and research will continue to determine its effectiveness beyond digital formative assessments.

REFERENCES

Beatty, B. J. (2019). *Hybrid-flexible course design* (1st ed.). EdTech Books. https://edtechbooks.org/pdfs/print/hyflex/_hyflex.pdf

Brown, A., & Green, T. (2017). Beyond teaching instructional design models: Exploring the design process to advance professional development and expertise. *Journal of Computing in Higher Education, 30*(1), 176–186.

Buchanan, T., Sainter, P., & Saunders, G. (2013). Factors affecting faculty use of learning technologies: Implications for models of technology adoption. *Journal of Computing in Higher Education 25*(1), 1–11.

Capp, M. (2017). The effectiveness of universal design for learning: A meta-analysis of literature between 2013–2016. *International Journal of Inclusive Education, 21*(8), 791–807.

Cohen, D., & Sasson, I. (2016). Online quizzes in a virtual learning environment as a tool for formative assessment. *Journal of Technology and Science Education, 6*(3), 188–208.

Darby, F., & Lang, J. (2019). *Small teaching online: Applying learning science in online classes.* John Wiley & Sons, Inc.

Davies, S., Mullan, J., & Feldman, P. (2017). Rebooting learning for the digital age: What next for technology-enhanced higher education? *Higher Education Policy Report, 93*, 1–58.

Deeley, S. (2017). Using technology to facilitate effective assessment for learning and feedback in higher education. *Assessment & Evaluation in Higher Education, 34*(3), 439–448.

Faber, J., Luyten, H., & Visscher, A. (2017). The effects of a digital formative assessment tool on mathematics achievement and student motivation: Results of a randomized experiment. *Computers & Education, 106*, 83–96.

Ghemawat, P. (2017). Strategies for higher education in the digital age. *California Management Review, 59*(4), 56–78.

Gikandi, J., Morrow, D., & Davis, N. (2011). Online formative assessment in higher education: A review of the literature. *Computers & Education, 57*, 2333–2351.

Gilboy, M. B., Heinerichs, S., & Pazzaglia, G. (2015). Enhancing student engagement using the flipped classroom. *Journal of Nutrition Education and Behavior, 47*(1), 109–114.

Heilporn, G., & Lakhal, S. (2021). Converting a graduate-level course into a HyFlex modality: What are effective engagement strategies? *The International Journal of Management Education, 19*(1), 100454.

King, E., & Boyatt, R. (2015). Exploring factors that influence adoption of e-learning within higher education. *British Journal of Educational Technology, 46*(6), 1272–1280.

Kopcha, T. J. (2012). Teachers' perceptions of the barriers to technology integration and practices with technology under situated professional development. *Computers & Education, 59*(4), 1109–1121.

Lapitan, L., Tiangco, C., Sumalinog, D., Sabarillo, N., & Diaz, J. (2021). An effective blended online teaching and learning strategy during the COVID-19 pandemic. *Education for Chemical Engineers, 35*, 116–131.

Loh, E. (2019). What we know about expectancy-value theory, and how it helps to design a sustained motivating learning environment. *System, 86*, 102–119.

Luo, T., Moore, D., & Franklin, T. (2019). Examining participation and engagement in a microblogging-supported college-level hybrid course. *Innovations in Education and Teaching International, 56*(1), 14–24.

Maier, U., Wolf, N., & Randler, C. (2016). Effects of a computer-assisted formative assessment intervention based on multiple-tier diagnostic items and different feedback types. *Computer & Education, 95*(2016), 85–98.

Mathies, C., & Ferland, C. (2017). Innovative strategic planning for the institution. In K. Powers & P. Schloss (Eds.), *Organization and administration in higher education* (pp. 105–122). Routledge.

McCarthy, J. (2017). Enhancing feedback in higher education: Students' attitudes towards online and in-class formative assessment feedback models. *Active Learning in Higher Education, 18*(2), 127–141.

McKenzie, L. (2018, July 10). *Canvas catches, and maybe passes, Blackboard*. Inside Higher Ed. https://insidehighered.com/digital-learning/article/2018/07/10/canvas-catches-and-maybe-passes-blackboard-top-learning.

Meer, N., & Chapman, A. (2014). Assessment for confidence: Exploring the impact that low-stakes assessment design has on student retention. *International Journal of Management Education, 12*(2), 186–192.

Melear, K. (2017). The role of internal governance, committees, and advisory groups. In K. Powers & P. Schloss (Eds.), *Organization and administration in higher education* (pp. 51–67). Routledge.

Panadero, E., Andrade, H., & Brookhart, S. (2018). Fusing self-regulated learning and formative assessment: A roadmap of where we are, how we got here, and where we are going. *The Australian Educational Researcher, 45*(1), 13–31.

Pearce, C. (2018). It pays to prepare: The value of low-stakes tutorial preparation exercises to student performance. *Australian Journal of Adult Learning, 58*(2), 246–265.

Petrovic, J., Pale, P., & Jeren, B. (2017). Online formative assessments in a digital signal processing course: Effects of feedback type and content difficulty on students learning achievements. *Education and Information Technologies, 22*(1), 3047–3061.

Polly, D., Martin, F., & Guilbaud, T. C. (2021). Examining barriers and desired supports to increase faculty members' use of digital technologies: Perspectives of faculty, staff, and administrators. *Journal of Computing in Higher Education, 33*, 135–156.

Porter, W., & Graham, C. (2016). Institutional drivers and barriers to faculty adoption of blended learning in higher education. *British Journal of Educational Technology, 47*(4), 748–762.

Pucciarelli, F., & Kaplan, A. (2016). Competition and strategy in higher education: Managing complexity and uncertainty. *Business Horizons, 59*(1), 311–320.

Reid, P. (2014). Categories for barriers to adoption of instructional technologies. *Education and Information Technologies, 19*(2), 383–407.

Reid, P. (2017). Supporting instructors in overcoming self-efficacy and background barriers to adoption. *Education and Information Technologies, 22*(1), 369–382.

Richardson, J., Ashby, I., Alshammari, A., Cheng, Z., Johnson, B., Krause, T., Lee, D., Randolph, A., & Wang, H. (2018). Faculty and instructional designers on building successful collaborative relationships. *Educational Technology Research and Development, 67*, 855–880.

Schneckenberg, D. (2010). Overcoming barriers for eLearning in universities—Portfolio models for eCompetence development of faculty. *British Journal of Educational Technology, 41*(6), 979–991.

Schrank, Z. (2016). An assessment of student perceptions and responses to frequent formative testing in introductory sociology classes. *Teaching Sociology, 44*(2), 118–127.

Sezen-Barrie, A., & Kelly, G. (2017). From the teacher's eyes: Facilitating teachers noticings on informal formative assessments (IFAs) and exploring the challenges to effective implementation. *International Journal of Science Education, 39*(2), 181–212.

Stringer, E. (2014). *Action research*. Sage Publications.

Wingo, N., Ivankova, N., & Moss, J. (2017). Faculty perceptions about teaching online: Exploring the literature using the technology acceptance model as an organizing framework. *Online Learning Journal, 21*(1), 15–35.

Xie, J., Gulinna, A., & Rice, M. (2021). Instructional designers' roles in emergency remote teaching during COVID-19. *Distance Education, 42*(1), 70–87.

Yee, K. (2015). Learner-centered faculty development. *New Directions for Teaching and Learning, 2015*(144), 99–107.

CHAPTER 2

BUILDING RELATIONSHIPS FOR SUCCESS

Exploring the Experiences of Students and Faculty in Postsecondary Developmental English Courses

Nicole Brewer

INTRODUCTION

Educators continue to search for ways to effectively redesign developmental English programs to benefit college students. These noncredit courses, which strengthen students' reading and writing skills, are often required courses designed to help underprepared students develop the skills they need to succeed in college level classes. At first glance, offering these courses can seem like a sufficient way to expand access to postsecondary education, yet the number of students who are required to take developmental education courses is high. According to a report by the U.S. Department of Education (2017), about one third of first-year students at undergraduate institutions enrolled in a developmental education course in 2011–2012. Furthermore, the completion and graduation rates for students who take these classes tend to be low. For example, only 5% of these students at two-year institutions graduate on time while just 20% of these students at most four-year institutions graduate on time (*Data dashboard*, 2017). The students who do persist through the required sequences of developmental education courses spend more time and money earning their degree than students who are not required to take these courses (Martinez & Bain, 2014).

Colleges and universities across the nation continue to implement a variety of changes designed to improve the completion and retention rates for students who take developmental education courses. These changes include cost reducing measures such as seeking grant funding and integrating technology, revising curriculum, changing placement measures, offering additional student support methods, and decreasing class size (Barhoum, 2018; Goldwasser et al., 2017). While these efforts result in some improvement, the problem of student retention persists. For example, a study on the success of learning communities for developmental education students found that the program improved course completion rates but did not significantly improve overall retention (Baier et al., 2019). Another study that measured the effectiveness of course redesigns and revised placement measures at five community colleges found that while students had higher GPAs, their rate of persistence did not significantly improve (Cooper et al., 2019).

Current efforts to redesign developmental education have not necessarily improved student outcomes in ways that are most meaningful: retention and graduation rates. As the efforts for the revision of developmental education continue, researchers, educators, and administrators are looking for more innovative ways to improve student outcomes. Since retention and graduation rates for students who take developmental education courses remain low, a shift away from focusing on structural revision methods is necessary.

The action research study discussed in this chapter explored the reasons for low course completion and retention rates for students who take developmental English courses at an open enrollment private university in New England. This action research study aimed to discover the reasons for these low course completion and retention rates and determine student support methods that could be used to improve these rates.

BACKGROUND AND CONTEXT

The existing literature on developmental English reform focuses on three key areas: structural modifications, pedagogical changes, and relationship building. The categorization of these areas was informed by Barhoum's (2017) framework for developmental writing reform. Barhoum's (2017) framework identifies four domains for promising practices in the field (structural, curricular, andragogical, and relational) and provides a useful foundation for understanding the current research interests and reform efforts in developmental education at postsecondary institutions.

Structural modifications include revising and eliminating the use of high-stake standardized tests to determine students' placement (Goldwasser et al., 2017;

Mokher et al., 2021; Woods et al., 2018), introducing accelerated or co-requisite courses into the programs instead of solely using standard, standalone developmental courses (Adams et al., 2009; Goldwasser, et al., 2017; Jenkins et al., 2010; Kallison, 2017), and constructing learning communities for additional support to students enrolled in these courses (Baker & Pomerantz, 2000; Baier et al., 2019; Pierce, 2017; Weiss et al., 2015). Structural changes, often the easiest of all reform efforts to enact (Barhoum, 2017, 2018), have been the primary focus of researchers and higher education leaders. While the existing literature supports the claim that structural reforms can improve academic outcomes for students, these studies have not shown conclusive evidence of a positive impact on student retention (Adams et al., 2009; Baker & Pomerantz, 2000; Kallison, 2017; Park-Gaghan et al., 2020; Weiss et al., 2015).

Pedagogical changes are associated with teaching and curriculum. They include the use of contextualized learning, in which students learn in relation to real-life situations, (Callahan & Chumney, 2009; Rochford, 2013; Zimmerer et al., 2018), a focus on metacognition, in which students gain an awareness of their own thinking processes, (Greci, 2019; Kallison, 2017; Pacello, 2019; Pierce, 2017), and movement away from the traditional "drill and skill" methods of teaching (Callahan & Chumney, 2009; Perun, 2015; Salyers, 2012). Pedagogical changes move away from the traditional model of teaching grammar and mechanics to prepare students for college coursework and are less researched than the more prevalent structural changes in developmental education (Barhoum, 2017, 2018). These reforms focus on what and how students are learning in the classroom instead of focusing on the placement testing and course format associated with the structural reforms.

Reform efforts related to building relationships or making connections involve recognizing the educational inequities for underserved student populations (Cantor, 2019; Mourad & Hong, 2017; Yue et al., 2018), working to improve student-instructor relationships (Brown, 2020; Moreno, 2015; Relles & Duncheon, 2018; Salyers, 2012), and acknowledging the importance of students' lived experiences (Perun, 2015; Relles & Duncheon, 2018; Salyers, 2012). Relational reform efforts consider the connections students make with faculty, staff, and other students and the effect those connections have on their academic progress and are explored the least in the literature on developmental education (Barhoum, 2017, 2018). Investigating these reform efforts are complex because they explore how human beings interact; however, since the problem of retention for students enrolled in developmental English courses persists, more research on reform related to relationship building is warranted. This study examined this least explored area of developmental education reform.

METHODS

This study was conducted at an open enrollment private university in New England serving a student body of approximately 3,200 students. While campus housing is available, most students are commuter students. The career-focused institution offers certificate, associate, baccalaureate, and master's degree programs. Some of the programs offered are in business, manufacturing, education, nursing, and the health sciences. About 50% of the student body identify as students of color, and 80% are women. Over 65% are first-generation students and nearly 70% of the student population is 25 years old or older.

Participants

The participants for Cycle 1 of this study were faculty and students. The participation criteria for faculty included working as an instructor (either part-time or full-time) at the university and experience teaching a developmental English course. The participation criteria for students included matriculating at the university and successfully completing a developmental English course. Judgment sampling, as described by Harrell and Bradley (2009), was used to recruit faculty participants. Faculty who fit the criteria were invited to participate in the study by email. Student participants were identified using the university's student information system. They were also identified using snowball sampling (Auerbach & Silverstein, 2003), in which faculty participants identified students who fit the inclusion criteria. All students were invited to participate using a recruitment email. For Cycle 1, the faculty participant sample consisted of six faculty, one part-time and five full-time. There was one student participant.

The participants for Cycle 2 were faculty and staff. The participant criteria for faculty and staff were working as full-time faculty or staff and regularly encountering or working with developmental English students. Faculty and staff participants for Cycle 2 were recruited using judgment sampling and snowball sampling. After consulting with administrators at the university, the researcher identified faculty and staff who fit the inclusion criteria and sent recruitment emails to them. Additional staff participants were identified using snowball sampling, through which potential staff participants identified other university staff who fit the inclusion criteria for Cycle 2 participants.

There were nine Cycle 2 participants for this study consisting of four faculty members and five staff members. The faculty participants were full-time faculty from various academic disciplines. The staff members were academic advisors and student affairs specialists or administrators.

Data Collection

Cycle 1 data were collected through 60-minute individual semi-structured interviews. Faculty interviews were conducted through video conference software; the student interview was conducted via phone. The interview protocol's focus for faculty was faculty's understanding of students' experiences and the effect the experiences had on students' ability to succeed in developmental English courses. The interview protocol for students focused on students' lived experiences. Faculty and students were asked about the perceived challenges to academic success and the perceived behaviors and attitudes that contributed to positive academic achievements. These semi-structured interviews gave further context concerning the action research study's central question.

The data collected during the first cycle informed the Cycle 2 data collection and action step for this research study. The action step for this research study was the co-creation of a committee of faculty and staff that had the goal of evaluating the student support methods utilized at the research site and developing a set of support methods to be implemented at the site that addressed the reasons for low course completion rates and retention rates described in the Cycle 1 interviews. The data for Cycle 2 were collected through a series of four 60-minute committee meetings and one focus group conducted through video conferencing software during the Fall 2021 semester. The four committee meetings were themed and were given titles related to those themes: (1) Understanding Our Students, (2) Evaluating Our Current Support Methods, (3) Developing and Revising Our Support Methods, and (4) Creating a Plan for Implementation. During these meetings, participants reviewed and discussed the data collected during Cycle 1 of the study as well as shared their own experiences working with students who had taken developmental English classes at the research site.

As a result of these four themed meetings, the participants co-created a set of five support methods to be implemented at the university to address the problem of low course completion rates and retention rates for students who take developmental English courses (Table 2). After the first four meetings, the faculty and staff participants took part in a focus group in which they evaluated their experience working on the semester-long committee. In addition to delivering the action step for this action research study, a set of five student support methods, the committee meetings conducted during Cycle 2 gave further information concerning the study's central problem of low course completion and retention rates for students who take developmental English courses.

Data Analysis

Interview and focus group transcripts, fieldnotes, and analytic memos were coded using several cycles of coding. In Vivo coding was used because of its unique capability to incorporate the voices of study participants (Saldaña, 2016). The choice to use In Vivo coding aligns with one of the action research study's focuses which is to understand how the experiences of students, staff, and faculty relate to students' academic outcomes. The coding process was conducted using word processing and spreadsheet software. During the Cycle 1 and Cycle 2 data analysis processes, series of codes were developed into categories and then distilled into relevant themes. The themes developed from Cycle 1 and Cycle 2 presented in this chapter explore the problem of low course completion and retention rates for students who take developmental English courses at the research site.

Trustworthiness

Trustworthiness was ensured through methods developed by both Lincoln and Guba (1985) and Shenton (2004). Credibility, transferability, dependability, and confirmability were addressed to determine trustworthiness. The researcher used prolong engagement to address credibility (Shenton, 2004) by gaining a familiarity with the research site through interviews with faculty members, observations of department meetings, and document analysis of course syllabi. Transferability was addressed through detailed explanations and descriptions of data collection methods, participants, and data analysis procedures (Shenton, 2004) to assist with the application of this qualitative study in similar contexts. Clear descriptions of the research design and the data collection process for both Cycles 1 and 2 assisted with dependability (Shenton, 2004). Confirmation was addressed through member checking (Lincoln & Guba, 1985) in which findings were shared with Cycle 1 and Cycle 2 participants using data displays, audio-visual presentations, and discussions with faculty at the research site knowledgeable about developmental English.

FINDINGS

The findings from this study suggested a variety of complex themes related to the low course completion and retention rates for students who take developmental English courses at this private open enrollment university in New England. While additional themes related to low course completion and retention rates emerged from the data analysis process, the themes discussed in this chapter are the themes most relevant to the relationship building realm of developmental education reform, the least often explored realm.

Cycle 1 Findings

The Cycle 1 findings for this action research study were categorized into four different reason-types: (1) interpersonal or intrapersonal reasons (2) sociocultural and socioeconomic reasons, (3) pedagogical reasons, and (4) institutional reasons (see Table 2.1). However, the first reason-type, interpersonal or intrapersonal reasons, is the only one explored in this chapter. The exploration of interpersonal and intrapersonal reasons gives a deeper understanding of challenges related to the relational realm (students building relationships with faculty, staff or other students) that students in developmental English courses face that directly or indirectly affect their ability to complete courses and persist.

Interpersonal or Intrapersonal Reasons

Interpersonal or intrapersonal reasons are factors that relate to a students' ability to create meaningful connections with others and their capacity to recognize their own capabilities and understand their sense of self. Students' sense of self, understanding of their abilities, and confidence in their own capabilities are all

TABLE 2.1. Themes from Cycle 1 Participant Interviews: Reasons for Low Completion and Retention Rates

Reason-Type	Definition	Example Quote
Interpersonal or intrapersonal	Factors related to relationship and connection building or related to students' sense of self that affect students' ability to persist in courses	"If you have a good professor, you'll get through it. It all depends on the professor. Because I told you my first math [class] was horrible... It was a disaster. It all depends [on] if you have the chemistry with the teacher" – Student
Sociocultural or socioeconomic	Events and circumstances that occur outside the classroom that can positively or negatively affect students' academic progress	"Every semester that I have taught [the developmental education cohort program], a student has told me that they are homeless. Without... exception, every single semester. There's been a student who is homeless for whatever reason and asked for help. Which, that's probably been the biggest, most difficult one. Other things ...have been food, you know, food insecurity, students who have been concerned about violence." – Faculty
Pedagogical	Factors related to the practice of teaching and learning that can influence student achievement	"You know, some students really liked the readings [even though] I think they may not necessarily have enjoyed reading. They liked what the story was; they connected to the story. And it resonated with them." – Faculty
Institutional	Factors associated with institutional policies and procedures that affect how students perform	"The other thing is really do these remedial classes really help? I'm wondering. Sometimes it's a waste of time and money. You know, ... [I] don't really think that's a reflection of how students really are. Like, I've made the Dean's list every semester. And I don't know, if honestly, if remedial classes actually helped that or not." – Student

related to interpersonal or intrapersonal reasons. Faculty participants stressed the importance of students not only understanding their capabilities but also feeling confident enough to use their skills successfully. One faculty member stated,

> And I cannot stress enough how important confidence in students [is]. And if they haven't been in school for a long time, if they've been told they're not good enough, if they, you know, that's all they need is confidence.

Interpersonal or intrapersonal reasons are also associated with the connections students make while taking courses. More specifically, the positive connections students make with their instructors better assist students in achieving their academic goals. When describing the environment of her classroom, one faculty member emphasized the importance of connection for students taking developmental education courses:

> So, while waiting for everyone to come in [to the classroom at the start of class], we kind of talk about how everyone is doing and really develop that, that connection, that relationship. So, they could get to...have somebody that they can talk to and someone they could, I don't want to say confide in, but just make a connection with because a lot of the students, especially in this population, need a connection with someone, whether it's a teacher, an advisor, or something.

It is also imperative to note that while a strong student-instructor connection can have a positive effect on students' experiences, the lack of connection can have a negative effect on students' achievement. The Cycle 1 student participant in the study candidly stated,

> if you have a good professor, you'll get through it. It all depends on the professor. Because [as] I told you, my first math [class] was horrible... It was a disaster. It all depends [on] if you have the chemistry with the teacher.

Cycle 2 Findings

Based on the Cycle 1 findings, the researcher developed an action step to directly address the problem of low course completion rates and retention rates for students who take developmental English courses at the research site. That action step involved the co-creation of a committee of faculty and staff who met four times during the Fall 2021 semester at the research site. The product of these committee meetings was the co-creation of five support methods to be implemented at the university to support students who take developmental English courses. These five support methods were (1) Extend Social Media Presence, (2) Information Technology Training for Students, (3) Adjunct Instructor On-Boarding, (4) Coffee with Faculty, and (5) the Writing Center (see Table 2).

Instead of focusing solely on further understanding the problem of low course completion and retention rates at the university, the Cycle 2 findings, which came as a result of the action step, creating five student support methods, focus on possible solutions for low course completion and retention rates The relevant findings from the Cycle 2 portion of this action research study have been categorized into the three different themes that are most relevant to providing solutions to the problem: (1) connection, (2) communication, and (3) collaboration.

Connection

This theme of connection, which can be described as the relationships faculty and staff create with students at the university, is directly related to the interpersonal and intrapersonal reasons discussed in the Cycle 1 findings. The Cycle 2 faculty and staff participants continually discussed the importance of building connections for students enrolled in the university's developmental English courses. During the first committee meeting, one faculty participant described how positive interpersonal relationships can enhance students' intrapersonal relationships:

> You, [an instructor], go into an English class, perhaps wrongly thinking, you're there to teach writing, but you very quickly learn that you have to teach your students all sorts of things right down to the level of how to find confidence in themselves as a person, both professionally and in their lives.

The participants' common understanding that building connections could positively influence the academic progress of students enrolled in developmental English led them to draft implementation plans for student support methods that encourage connection building. One of the methods the participants titled, *Coffee with Faculty*. Coffee with Faculty is a student support method that facilitates regular gatherings with faculty and students, at which students can meet with faculty teaching developmental English courses and other faculty to build stronger, more meaningful relationships outside of the classroom. One faculty participant expressed that Coffee with Faculty, "kind of helps to build a sense of, you know, rapport between the instructors and students. I think especially the developmental level, that might be really impactful."

Communication

Communication refers to the ability to successfully communicate ideas, concepts, and information to others. Communication in this context not only refers to students' ability to communicate with faculty and staff, but also to the institution's ability to effectively communicate important information to students. While the participants were concerned with the students' ability to communicate with their instructors and staff members in order to receive appropriate support, participants also recognized that the institution did not always communicate effectively with students. The COVID-19 pandemic exposed the ways in which institutional communication at the institution could be ineffective, as highlighted by one staff participant:

> So, while we know that everything remained the same [when the university placed restrictions due to COVID-19], and ... they [support services] were online, ... I think that because students just physically couldn't see a tutor or walk in and make an appointment, they just thought it wasn't there.

While the institution was disseminating important information to the student body, the participants recognized that students were not always accessing that information. To improve the effectiveness of communication at the university to support students enrolled in developmental English courses, the participants drafted an implementation plan designated, *Information Technology Training for Students*. This support method involved creating an IT training module for new students at the university. This module, which would be a required noncredit training module, was developed by the participants to improve students' understanding of technology and improve their ability to effectively communicate. One staff participant suggested that IT training for students could improve the all-school communications by encouraging students to more regularly use their student email, the primary way faculty, staff, and the institution communicate with students: "I think that, you know, the communication is going to improve if we all agree to use one tool to communicate with students."

Collaboration

Collaboration, which can be described as faculty and staff members' ability to work together on institutional projects, is the last theme that emerged from the Cycle 2 data findings. This final theme does not refer to the way in which faculty and staff work directly with students. Instead, it highlights the way in which the interactions among faculty and staff can significantly influence students' academic experiences. One staff participant suggested that improving faculty and staff collaboration could increase student use of academic support methods:

> Because often when we tell students, "Hey, we have this writing center, or hey, we have this resource you should go," ... they typically don't go on their own. ... So, maybe if we start that introduction, or bring the class to the center [Writing Center], they'll feel more comfortable going.

The participants developed a student support method that related to the importance of increased collaboration among faculty and staff: the Writing Center. While the Writing Center was already in existence at the time of the action research study, faculty and staff participants proposed a more active one that served the entire student body. For developmental English students, a more active writing center would mean increased support not only while students were enrolled in developmental English courses but also more importantly when they began taking college level courses that required academic writing. One faculty participant stated in relation to supporting the Writing Center:

> The key thing with tutors in a writing center or study groups [is] they meet students where they are with their specific needs... It doesn't matter really what the student's needs are. [They] are going to be addressed... It's for all levels, you know, this is not just a resource built for developmental classes. This is one that will support all English classes.

In terms of collaboration, the Cycle 2 participants believed that an active writing center with a strong campus presence, which supports developmental English students throughout their entire time at the university, would require the collaboration of faculty and staff to be effective. One faculty participant described the level of collaboration needed to maintain an active Writing Center:

> There's a lot of work to be done in terms of forging the support connections between faculty and administration, ensuring that we have the space figuring out the schedule of who's going to staff it, what faces are going to be there on a regular basis.

Finally, the design of this action research study, which required faculty and staff to work together to co-create plans over the course of an academic semester, also allowed for further exploration of the impact that faculty and staff collaboration can have on students' success. In the focus group, which was held once the committee meetings concluded, the Cycle 2 faculty and staff participants noted that the structure of the committee meetings fostered collaboration. One staff participant stated:

> I really appreciated how there was both staff and faculty members and bringing different sides of the house, really, in so that everybody could add input to make this as holistic as possible. So, I thought it was really great that we got a lot of different opinions, ideas.

The faculty and staff participants continually discussed how student supports needed effective collaboration among faculty and staff to successfully serve the developmental English student population.

DISCUSSION

The findings of this action research study contribute to the literature on developmental education at postsecondary institutions by exploring the ways in which student support methods that focus on relationship building among faculty, staff, and students can impact course completion and retention rates for students who enroll in developmental English courses. First, this action research study supports the body of literature that recognizes that fostering strong relationships and building connections for students enrolled in developmental education courses can positively influence students' experiences in higher education (Callahan & Chumney, 2009; Relles & Duncheon, 2018; Salyers, 2012). In their study in which they explored how developmental English classrooms were influenced by institutional policies and structures, Relles and Duncheon (2018) noted that instructor-student interaction, particularly an instructor's ability to use informal discourse to create a supportive classroom environment, helped students feel more connected to the social community and build a more positive outlook. Similarly, Salyers' (2012) research study, which analyzed the effect that an academic listening exercise had on students in a developmental English class, recognized the significance that social and cultural barriers have on student learning. A study conducted by Callahan and Chumney (2009), which compared the experiences of students in a developmental English course at a community college to those of students in a developmental English course at a research university acknowledged that effective developmental courses do not just fill in learning gaps but also help students develop confidence and self-sufficiency. This research study demonstrates the importance of relationship building to student success, especially for students enrolled in developmental education programs.

Furthermore, this study supports the findings from other research studies that highlight the positive effect that community building can have on students' success (Baker & Pomerantz, 2000; Yue et al., 2018). A study by Baker and Pomerantz (2000) on the impact of learning communities on students' academic success at a commuter college found students involved in learning communities were more engaged, which had a positive impact on their learning experience. In a study conducted by Yue et al. (2018) that explored how supplemental instruction affected students' success in a developmental course, the researchers concluded that the social interaction facilitated by supplemental instruction encouraged students to develop a sense of belonging that contributed to closing the performance gap between disadvantaged students and non-disadvantaged students.

Secondly, the results of this study provide another area of developmental education research that can be further explored. The theme of collaboration, which emerged as part of the Cycle 2 data collection process, suggests the importance of the work that faculty and staff do together to successfully support students enrolled in developmental English courses. While the significance of collaboration is discussed in some studies on developmental education (Relles & Duncheon, 2018; Schrynemakers et al., 2019; Williams et al., 2018), the impact collaboration or lack thereof has on students' academic experiences is less often explored. The study by Relles and Duncheon (2018) implies the need for stronger collaboration among faculty and administration when the researchers suggest that institutions consider how their policies and structures undermine the success of students and ability of instructors to perform. Similarly, a study by Schrynemakers et al. (2019), in which the researchers aim to learn more about faculty's perceptions about students' readiness after developmental education reforms at a set of community colleges, recommends faculty involvement in policy changes to improve faculty perceptions of developmental education reform efforts. Finally, a study by Williams et al. (2018) intended to understand high school teachers' perceptions of developmental education in higher education recommends the need for collaboration among high school teachers and college faculty, highlighting a lack of communication between high schools and colleges, which could influence the success of students enrolled in developmental education courses.

It must be noted that the impact of collaboration in higher education has been thoroughly explored (Kezar, 2005; Kochan & Mullen, 2010; Macfarlane, 2017; Magolda, 2001; Newell & Bain, 2020). However, the impact of collaboration in higher education specifically related to developmental education is much less often explored. The results of this research study suggest that faculty-staff collaboration could facilitate academic success for students enrolled in developmental English courses.

As the action research study described in this chapter implies, cross-department collaboration may not only help note inefficacies in current institutional operations, but it may also encourage innovative problem-solving to better serve students. Since much of the research on developmental education refers to the impact of the work and support services beyond the instructors inside the classroom (Callahan & Chumney, 2009; Goldwasser et al., 2017; Moreno & Rutledge, 2018; Perun, 2015; Rochford, 2013; Schrynemakers et al., 2019; Yue et al., 2018), this action research study's focus on collaboration represents a logical progression for developmental education research: developmental education research could benefit from focusing on the effect that faculty-staff collaboration has on improving completion and retention rates for students taking developmental education courses.

LIMITATIONS

There are four significant limitations to this action research study. First, while the findings of this action research project can give insight into developmental English programs in higher education settings, the results cannot be generalized to other institutions. Secondly, this study lacks ample representation of students' voices. Recruiting students who had successfully passed a developmental English course was difficult. In addition, finding students who had not only successfully passed a class, but also had the time and ability to speak with the researcher for an hour interview was challenging. A third limitation of this study was that it was conducted during the COVID-19 pandemic. Safety protocols only allowed for virtual interviews. Faculty participants were able to adjust to the virtual interview format, but students were less able to do so. In addition, fewer students were enrolling in developmental English courses while the research site was offering only remote learning options for students. This narrowed the participant pool. The final significant limitation of this study was that the developmental English program was in transition at the research site during the time of the study. The curriculum and placement methods for the program were being revised, which also influenced the nature of the student participant pool.

IMPLICATIONS FOR PRACTICE

The findings of this action research study suggest some implications for practice. This action research study focuses on the act of building connections and how connection building among faculty, staff, and students can impact student success in the developmental English classroom. While structural changes, such as revising course placement methods or redesigning course models, and pedagogical changes, such as the use of contextual learning, show promise in increasing students' academic performance, institutions of higher education may also benefit from implementing student support methods that aim to help students make more meaningful and lasting connections during their studies. Connection building could have an impact on student retention, thus giving students more support to persist toward graduation. Faculty, staff, and administrators should consider how the courses, activities, and policies they create enhance or hinder students' ability to build meaningful connections on campus. Connection building as an intentional practice could have a lasting positive effect for all students but especially vulnerable student populations, such as students enrolled in developmental courses.

This action research study's focus on the relational realm, which refers to the connections that students, faculty, and staff make with one another, also has specific implications for the way in which practitioners collaborate. The ability of faculty and staff to communicate and work together effectively could have a significant effect on the experiences of students. Institutions that encourage an environment in which faculty and staff members have strong working relationships may improve the efficiency of student support methods and even create the opportunity for innovation. As much of the literature on collaboration in higher education suggests, shifting the higher education landscape to support collaboration can be extremely challenging. However, facilitating this shift in an institution's environment may improve students' academic experience. The importance of faculty, staff, and administration to collaborate effectively should not be overlooked. When new courses, policies, and initiatives are implemented, institutions should prioritize collaboration to better ensure that students will be well-supported.

REFERENCES

Adams, P., Gearhart, S., Miller, R., & Roberts, A. (2009). *The accelerated learning program: Throwing open the gates*. City University of New York.

Auerbach, C. F., & Silverstein, L. B. (2003). *Qualitative data: An introduction to coding and analysis*. New York University.

Baier, S. T., Gonzales, S. M., & Sawilowsky, S. S. (2019). Classroom learning communities' impact on students in developmental courses. *Journal of Developmental Education, 42*(3), 2–28.

Baker, S., & Pomerantz, N. (2000). Impact of learning communities on retention at a metropolitan university. *Journal of College Student Retention: Research, Theory & Practice, 2*(2), 115–126. https://doi.org/10.2190/62P5-CQ2U-NTUW-DM1C

Barhoum, S. (2017). Community college developmental writing programs most promising practices: What the research tells educators. *Community College Journal of Research and Practice, 41*(12), 791–808. https://doi.org/1080/10668926.2016.1231092

Barhoum, S. (2018). Increasing student success: Structural recommendations for community colleges. *Journal of Developmental Education, 41*(3), 18–25.

Brown, C. A. (2020). The impact of inclusiveness and rurality in developmental student writing needs and curricular responses: A Pasifika community college case study. *Journal of Alternative Perspectives in the Social Sciences, 10*(4), 763–791.

Callahan, N., & Chumney, D. (2009). Write like college: How remedial writing courses at a community college and a research university position at-risk students in the field of higher education. *Teachers College Record, 111*(7), 1619–1664.

Cantor, M. R. (2019). Retention of long island millennials at a suburban community college: Are they college ready? *Journal for Leadership and Instruction, 18*(1), 36–41.

Cooper, E. E., McGee, J. R., Levine-Brown, P., & Bolt, L. (2019). The effectiveness of redesigns in developmental education. *Journal of Developmental Education, 43*(1), 20–32.

Data dashboard. (2017, March 28). Complete College America. https://completecollege.org/data-dashboard/

Goldwasser, M., Martin, K., & Harris, E. (2017). A framework for assessing developmental education programs. *Journal of Developmental Education, 40*(2), 10.

Greci, D. (2019). Reading expectations and text readiness in 100-level courses. *Journal of Developmental Education, 42*(3), 18–26.

Harrell, M. C., & Bradley, M. A. (2009). *Data collection methods. Semi-structured interviews and focus groups*. Rand National Defense Research Institute

Jenkins, D., Speroni, C., Belfield, C., Jaggars, S. S., & Edgecombe, N. (2010, September). *A model for accelerating academic success of community college remedial English students: Is the Accelerated Learning Program (ALP) effective and affordable?* (CCRC Working Paper No. 21). Community College Research Center. https://ccrc.tc.columbia.edu/media/k2/attachments/remedial-english-alp-effective-affordable.pdf

Kallison, J. M. (2017). The effects of an intensive postsecondary transition program on college readiness for adult learners. *Adult Education Quarterly, 67*(4), 302–321. https://doi.org/10.1177/0741713617725394

Kezar, A. (2005, November 1). Moving from I to, reorganizing for collaboration in higher education. *Change: The Magazine of Higher Learning, 37*(6), 50–57. https://doi.org/10.3200/CHNG.37.6.50-57

Kochan, F. K., & Mullen, C. A. (2010). An exploratory study of collaboration in higher education from women's perspectives. *Teaching Education, 14*(2), 153–167. https://doi.org/10.1080/1047621032000092959

Lincoln, Y. S., & Guba, E. G. (1985). *Naturalistic Inquiry*. Sage Publications.

Macfarlane, B. (2017). The paradox of collaboration: A moral continuum. *Higher Education Research & Development, 36*(3), 472–485. https://doi.org/10.1080/07294360.2017.1288707

Magolda, P. (2001). Border crossings: Collaboration struggles in education. *The Journal of Educational Research, 94*(6), 346–358. http://www.jstor.org.ezproxy.neu.edu/stable/27542346

Martinez, M. E., & Bain, S. F. (2014, February). The costs of remedial and developmental education in postsecondary education. *Research in Higher Education Journal, 22*(1), 1–12.

Mokher, C. G., Park-Gaghan, T. J., & Hu, S. (2021). What happens to efficiency and equity? the cost implications of developmental education reform. *Research in Higher Education, 62*(2), 151–174. https://doi.org/10.1007/s11162-020-09593-w

Moreno, G. A. (2015). Making meaning about educational experiences through participatory action research: A project conducted with adults enrolled in a community college mathematics course. *Educational Action Research, 23*(2), 178–193. https://doi.org/10.1080/09650792.2014.980285

Moreno, G. A., & Rutledge, D. (2018). A response to strategies and tactics through participatory action research in a developmental mathematics course. *Educational Action Research, 26*(3), 420–438. https://doi.org/10.1080/09650792.2017.1351384

Mourad, R., & Hong, J. H. (2017). Comparison of developmental student outcomes in college level courses using propensity score matching. *Journal of Applied Research in the Community College, 24*(1), 59–76.

Newell, C., & Bain, A. (2020). Academics' perceptions of collaboration in higher education course design. *Higher Education Research & Development, 39*(4), 748–763. https://doi.org/10.1080/07294360.2019.1690431

Pacello, J. (2019). Developmental writing and transfer: Examining student perceptions. *Journal of Developmental Education, 42*(3), 10–17.

Park-Gaghan, T. J., Mokher, C. G., Hu, X., Spencer, H., & Hu, S. (2020). What happened following comprehensive developmental education reform in the Sunshine State? The impact of Florida's developmental education reform on introductory college-level course completion. *Educational Researcher*. https://doi.org/10.3102/0013189X20933876

Perun, S. A. (2015). What the hell is revise? *Community College Review, 43*(3), 245–263. https://doi.org/10.1177/0091552115580593

Pierce, C. A. (2017). Research-based integrated reading and writing course development. *Journal of Developmental Education, 40*(2), 23.

Relles, S. R., & Duncheon, J. C. (2018). Inside the college writing gap: Exploring the mixed messages of remediation support. *Innovative Higher Education, 43*(3), 217–231.

Rochford, R. A. (2013). Service-learning for remedial reading and writing students. *Null, 37*(5), 345–355. https://doi.org/10.1080/10668926.2010.532463

Saldaña, J. (2016). *The coding manual for qualitative researchers*. SAGE Publications.

Salyers, S. (2012). Formal English without tears: Rewriting the narrative of the "low-level" learner. *Educational Journal of Living Theories, 5*(1), 67–91.

Schrynemakers, I., Lane, C., Beckford, I., & Kim, M. (2019). College readiness in post-remedial academia: Faculty observations from three urban community colleges. *Community College Enterprise, 25*(1), 10–31.

Shenton, A. K. (2004). Strategies for ensuring trustworthiness in qualitative research projects. *Education for Information, 22*(2), 63–75. https://doi-org.ezproxy.neu.edu/10.3233/EFI-2004-22201

U.S. Department of Education. (2017, January). *Developmental education: Challenges and strategies for reform*. U.S. Department of Education, Office of Planning, Evaluation, and Policy Development.

Weiss, M. J., Visher, M. G., Weissman, E., & Wathington, H. (2015). The impact of learning communities for students in developmental education: A synthesis of findings from randomized trials at six community colleges. *Educational Evaluation and Policy Analysis, 37*(4), 520–541. https://doi.org/10.3102/0162373714563307

Williams, M. R., Tompkins, P., & Rogers, B. (2018). High school teachers' perceptions of developmental education. *Journal of Developmental Education, 41*(2), 2–11.

Woods, C. S., Park, T., Hu, S., & Betrand Jones, T. (2018). How high school coursework predicts introductory college-level course success. *Community College Review, 46*(2), 176–196. https://doi.org/10.1177/0091552118759419

Yue, H., Rico, S. R., Vang, M. K., & Giuffrida, T. A. (2018). Supplemental instruction: Helping disadvantaged students reduce performance gap. *Journal of Developmental Education, 41*(2), 18–25.

Zimmerer, M., Skidmore, S. T., Chuppa-Cornell, K., Sindel-Arrington, T., & Beilman, J. (2018). Contextualizing developmental reading through information literacy. *Journal of Developmental Education, 41*(3), 2–8.

CHAPTER 3

A DIGITAL COMMUNITY OF CONNECTIONS FOR PART-TIME TEACHER EDUCATORS

One Educator's Growth

Jodie Donner

In learning, the present powers of the pupil are the initial stage; the aim of the teacher represents the remote limit. Between the two lie means—that is middle conditions:—acts to be performed; difficulties to be overcome; appliances to be used. Only through them, in the literal time sense, will the initial activities reach a satisfactory consummation (Dewey, 1916, p. 149).

Educational philosopher John Dewey's description of a teacher's role in learning has remained much the same over a century after his visionary explanation of the learning process. Nevertheless, important differences exist in the 'means' and the 'appliances to be used.' Now, teachers must have become masters of technological pedagogy to ensure students achieve the 'remote limit,' which has altered how educators use instructional technology. Thus, teacher preparation programs have modified their curricular requirements and instructional approaches to pro-

---

Faculty Development: Achieving Change Through Action Research, pages 31–44.
Copyright © 2024 by Information Age Publishing
www.infoagepub.com
All rights of reproduction in any form reserved.

vide students with appropriate experiences addressing the continuously advancing 'means' encountered in classrooms.

These modern 'middle conditions' have been replete with technological tools and myriad related instructional methods, which have led to national standards guiding teachers as they develop appropriately aligned pedagogy to support students' learning opportunities. Likewise, programs preparing educators for the field have employed methods consistent with the expectations and standards of national and local regulating entities. Not all programs, however, include sufficient training for their teacher educators (TEs) to effectively prepare their students to achieve the required standards. This was true of the teacher preparation program in the institution in which I served as a technology strategist.

BACKGROUND AND CONTEXT

Teacher preparation programs, such as those within Arizona State University's Mary Lou Fulton Teachers College (MLFTC), must meet accreditation standards and federal expectations. Accordingly, requirements included preparing teacher candidates (TCs) to teach with technology (Council for the Accreditation of Educator Preparation, 2013; Council of Chief State School Officers, 2013). Educator standards based on digital pedagogy from the International Society for Technology in Education (ISTE) are part of most programs as well (ISTE, 2017). Moreover, the United States Department of Education, Office of Educational Technology (OET, 2016) provided guidelines for programs to ensure TCs were "prepared to meaningfully incorporate technology into their practice immediately upon entering the classroom . . . trained by faculty using technology in transformative ways . . ." (p. 4).

Although those expectations exist, some teacher preparation programs fall short in providing their TCs with appropriate and consistent educational experiences leading their graduates to exit programs able to achieve effective technology integration. As defined, technology integration is using technologies in schools for student knowledge creation (Belland, 2009) and includes blending technology with pedagogy and content knowledge (Mishra & Koehler, 2006). Two primary factors have led to TCs graduating with incomplete technology integration mastery—an absence of sustained professional development (PD) for TEs and a notable percentage of part-time TEs, often with frequent turnover each term.

At this particular university, the college used a model called technology infusion (TInf), which embedded technology integration experiences in required content methods courses (Foulger et al., 2019). TInf was implemented in 2011 to prepare TCs to integrate technology in their teaching consistent with national standards and state requirements (Title 7, 2018). In prior work, TInf specialists working with TEs successfully infused technology into methods courses (Buss et al., 2015, 2018; Foulger et al., 2015, 2019; Wetzel et al., 2014) providing TCs with learning experiences to develop technology integration. The model produced positive results effective in aiding TEs to prepare TCs to teach with technology.

Despite these earlier successes with TInf, however, areas of concern did merit improvement. For example, a dedicated and sustainable PD program did not exist. One technology infusion specialist provided all related support and content development; whereas, in prior years, two or more staff members fulfilled the duties. An additional concern was the high proportion of part-time faculty associates (FAs), instructors with course loads of three or fewer courses. FAs were often new due to frequent turnover and had less access to professional development (PD). Therefore, student learning experiences provided by FAs may have differed from those offered by other TEs, especially full-time or those who had been with the college during the initial TInf implementation, possibly resulting in some TCs missing instruction and modeling required for them to graduate 'ready to teach with technology.' Instituting a facilitated online community of practice (OCoP; Wenger, 1998, 2009) could address these contextual issues as identified by other researchers who studied technology integration support needs and digital solutions providing connection and PD for educators (Buss et al., 2015, 2018; Dorner & Kumar, 2016; Foulger et al., 2015, 2017; Macià & García, 2016; Peeraer & Van Petegem, 2012; Smith et al., 2017; Wetzel et al., 2014).

METHODS

One of the largest teacher preparation programs in the United States, housed within a research university with a total of over 63,000 undergraduates, was the site of this study. Over 700 TCs graduate each academic year, and the total college enrollment is nearly 7,000 students. In fall 2020 37.8% of teacher preparation sections were staffed by FAs. Full-time faculty members who teach courses leading to teacher certification number 110. The college averages a pool of 180 FAs, which includes combinations of veteran and new instructors varying from semester to semester.

PARTICIPANTS

In cycle 1, participation criteria included instructors who were teaching courses both labeled as technology-infused and required in teacher preparation programs. This sample was limited, as these faculty members were certain to be teaching with technology, and might need support and PD. Using the participation criteria, I recruited instructors to voluntarily join the pilot. The final participant sample consisted of five participants. Three were FAs, and two were full-time TEs. Of the FAs, two were new to the college (including Jenn, a pseudonym, the focus of this case study) and one was a returner. One of the full-time faculty members had been with the college for multiple years, and the other was new.

For cycle 2, criteria for participation shifted to including FAs who were teaching technology-infused teacher preparation courses and faculty members who were serving as their mentors as part of a new support program (a mix of full- and part-time TEs). Various veteran, full-time faculty also participated and included faculty who were teaching courses leading to teacher certification. I recruited participants during the new faculty orientation session at the start of the semester. The final participant sample was 53 and was a combination of veteran and new FAs (including Jenn) and veteran and new full-time TEs.

Cycle 3 participant criteria included instructors who were part-time and teaching any course in teacher preparation. These criteria developed as previous cycles indicated all FAs could benefit, not just those in charge of technology-infused courses. This resulted in 111 total participants included in the intervention (along with three veteran, full-time faculty mentors) Jenn was again a participant and was in her third semester as an FA in the college.

DATA COLLECTION

Cycle 1 data included Canvas analytics exported from the LMS. Data described participants' time spent in the OCoP and which pages and content they accessed. Four participants also responded to four face-to-face interviews lasting between 20 and 30 minutes and using a semi-structured interview protocol. Questions related to participants' use, perception, and application of the OCoP.

For cycle 2, I employed a retrospective pre- and post-intervention structure measuring self-reported growth in three constructs: Technological Pedagogical Content Knowledge or TPACK (Mishra & Koehler, 2006), Teacher Educator Technology Competencies or TETCs (Foulger et al., 2017), and self-efficacy (Bandura, 1977, 1997). Participants responded to the retrospective pre-survey ($n = 12$) and one-week later responded to the post-survey ($n = 10$). The retrospective pre-survey also included open-ended items related to benefits, use, and evaluations of the OCoP. Three participants responded to questions about the OCoP's benefits, needs, and their use during 20–30-minute face-to-face interviews using a semi-structured interview protocol.

Cycle 3 data consisted of analytics from both Slack and Canvas. Slack data was anonymized, so provided an overall description of networking and communication among participants. Canvas data did describe participants' individual activities and access and included time spent in the Canvas portion of the OCoP and time spent on specific pages. Data also identified which pages participants visited. Participants responded again to the same retrospective pre-survey (n = 12) and one week later to the post-survey (n = 12). Additional qualitative data came from Canvas lesson observations (five lessons each from four FAs) using a protocol I derived from TPACK instrument items (Schmidt et al., 2009), ISTE Standards (ISTE, 2017), and Triple E lesson analysis rubrics (Kolb, 2017). Finally, eight FAs participated in Zoom interviews lasting about 30 minutes using a semi-structured interview protocol.

DATA ANALYSIS

Data analysis occurred throughout the study and included methods based on those described by Charmaz (2014), Saldaña (2016), Glaser and Strauss (1967), Greene (2007), and Creswell and Creswell (2018). I coded qualitative data using HyperResearch and constant comparative methods to develop categories, themes, then assertions. I produced descriptive statistics and a repeated measures analysis of variance (ANOVA) using SPSS (IBM SPSS Statistics, Version 25.0).

TRUSTWORTHINESS AND QUALITY ASSURANCE

A step toward enhancing trustworthiness and mitigation of limitations was using various data sources. In the study, I used multiple data sources to address validity and trustworthiness (Creswell & Creswell, 2018; Ivankova, 2015; Maxwell, 2013). Using surveys, interviews, Slack analytics, Canvas analytics, and observations of instructors' teaching materials with interpretative notes allowed me to determine whether these data display similar results, which is a method of increasing validity. This triangulation process allowed me to find common themes that substantiate each other, hence improving validity (Creswell & Creswell, 2018). I recognize the application of the lesson analysis protocol includes a subjective element. However, developing the protocol based on research (ISTE, 2017; Kolb, 2017; Schmidt et al., 2009) and analyzing my interpretive notes is evidence of working toward improving validity and credibility of the study. The constant comparative method and writing memos increases validity of qualitative interview data and results in definitive themes (Charmaz, 2014; Glaser & Strauss, 1967).

FINDINGS

Quantitative data from the paired retrospective, pre- and post-intervention scores indicated participants' TPACK, knowledge of technology (TETC), and self-efficacy scores increased significantly for the 12 participants who responded to both surveys in the final cycle, which included Jenn. Results have been presented in Table 3.1.

TABLE 3.1. Means and Standard Deviations* for Pre- and Post-Intervention Scores for the Three Dependent Variables from the Survey (n = 12)

Variable	Pre-Intervention Scores	Post-Intervention Scores
TPACK	4.73 (0.86)	5.49 (0.43)
TETC	3.75 (1.31)	4.78 (1.20)
Self-Efficacy	4.60 (0.99)	5.33 (0.46)

*Standard deviations have been presented in parentheses.

Canvas analytics revealed Jenn was active in the OCoP in both cycles with that data. During cycle 3, she engaged for 1238 minutes, equaling nearly 21 hours, and logged 362 page views. Slack data were anonymized, so describing Jenn's quantitative use was not possible. Nevertheless, she described her use, qualitatively, during her interview responses.

Jenn's interview responses, along with those of seven other participants, resulted in four themes and related assertions, developed through coding and codeweaving (Saldaña, 2016) of all interview participants' qualitative data. Themes, their corresponding theme-related components, and key assertions from the combined interview and open-ended responses data have been provided in Table 3.2.

Jenn noted her *technology integration*, theme 1, included engaging her students with different tools matching pedagogical purpose. Drawing upon her TPACK knowledge, she dismissed a tool because ." . . this would be something I was just adding rather than . . . part of the pedagogy and the content I was teaching." She also used tools others recommended in the OCoP. About tools mentioned in the OCoP, she said, "The Padlet . . . That's the one that stuck out because I really liked Padlet." Related to the second theme, *factors influencing her integration*, Jenn attended to her perceptions of students' needs, commenting she chose technology experiences to support her students. Specifically, Jenn said, "I really do like the

TABLE 3.2. Themes* and Theme-Related Components and Assertions

Themes and Theme-related Components		Assertions
Discussion of instructional technology integration 1. Experiences teaching with technology 2. Functional technology use 3. Instructional decisions 4. Identified limitations of technology	1.	Instructors balanced functional and pedagogical technology use as members of the OCoP, which affected their instructional decisions and responses to technology limitations.
Factors affecting technology use and integration 1. Focus on student needs 2. Recognition of personal limits 3. Feelings of support 4. Risk-taking to learn 5. Technology integration knowledge from familiar sources outside of the OCoP	2.	When planning pedagogical technology use, instructors relied upon various sources of knowledge as they attended to their personal limits and their students' needs.
Development of technology integration 1. Improved skills 2. Gained knowledge 3. Technology problem-solving through collaborations with others	3.	Instructors gained technology integration knowledge, improved technology skills, and applied their learning in their teaching experiences.
Online community of practice reflections 1. OCoP engagement levels 2. Reflection on OCoP engagement 3. Intention to revisit OCoP	4.	Instructors who engaged in the OCoP found it valuable and benefitted through identified knowledge gains, increases in self-efficacy, and elements of community.

*Note. Themes are in italics.

TABLE 3.3. Lesson Analyses Scores for Jenn

Lesson	Pedagogical Use	Skills	Self-efficacy
1	14	2	4
2	17	2	5
3	17	2	5
4	17	2	5
5	18	2	5

Note. Pedagogical Use max = 18, Skills max = 4, Self-efficacy max = 6

idea of Slack, but I didn't feel like the class was ready for it." About *developing her technology integration*, theme 3, Jenn said, "I've been a part of this [the OCoP] for the past four semesters. For me it [technology integration] comes quite naturally.... we were constantly using technology [in class]." *Reflecting on OCoP use*, which was the final theme, she said she read content in Canvas and Slack for hours each week and said the OCoP contributed to her teaching methods. About Slack, she noted, "I really liked reading what other people were doing."

Using the lesson analysis protocol I developed, analyses of Jenn's five lessons resulted in assigned scores for three constructs: pedagogical technology use, technology skills, and self-efficacy related to technology integration, presented in Table 3.3. Jenn's profile indicated a modest developmental pattern in all constructs except skills.

Coding (Saldaña, 2016) of the lesson analyses interpretive notes resulted in three orientations describing digital pedagogy: developing, adequate, highly-proficient. Jenn's orientation was adequate based on students' frequent and active technology uses, clear pedagogical technology strategies, and her levels of self-efficacy and modeling. Although Jenn integrated digital technologies in teaching and learning, she demonstrated some deficiencies, particularly with respect to skills.

DISCUSSION

Results of this study focus on Jenn's activity levels in the two digital spaces within the OCoP and resulting potential influences. Data describing Jenn's use of the OCoP intervention, her perceptions of the OCoP, and the potential effects of the intervention on her pedagogical technology use, technology skills, technology use, and self-efficacy result in three prominent findings. Discussion of the findings includes three sections: (a) Jenn reports and displays increases in technological integration, improvements in digital pedagogy, and increases in self-efficacy; (b) Jenn actively engages with the OCoP experience and consumes its content; and (c) Jenn's orientation level toward digital pedagogy may be due, in part, to her experiences with the OCoP. Related theoretical perspectives and literature connections are included in these sections.

Increases in Technological Integration, Digital Pedagogy, and Self-Efficacy

Results show substantial increases in skills and behaviors related to TPACK, TETCs, and self-efficacy. Taken together, the results of the anonymous retrospective, pre- and post-intervention surveys, which included Jenn's responses; and Jenn's interview data are evidence of growth related to teaching with technology and associated confidence. Therefore, Jenn's suspected gains in the three constructs of TPACK, TETCs, and self-efficacy and her intensive OCoP engagement point to the conclusion that participation in the OCoP affects increases in these areas. Likewise, Jenn mentions specific learning from the OCoP and attributes her improvements in these areas to her engagement with the OCoP.

Gains Jenn displays after participating in the OCoP match findings in related research. Notably, Macià and García (2016) also find teachers who are participants in online networking opportunities improve in areas related to PD and self-efficacy. Karam et al. (2018) observe similar results in their study of science teachers. Abbit's (2011) results also show a connection between TPACK (Mishra & Koehler, 2006) and self-efficacy (Bandura, 1977, 1997), which is consistent with the results in this study depicting increases in both constructs.

OCoP Engagement and Consumption

Responses in Jenn's interview and anonymous data from the retrospective, pre- and post-intervention surveys point to absorbing the OCoP content as affecting improvements in TPACK, TETCs, and self-efficacy. Jenn's reported use of the OCoP matches the analytical data available. Recall, she is active in the Canvas component for almost 21 hours. Although aggregated data from Slack was not available, Jenn comments she reads through the Slack posts and interacts with occasional comments or with emoji to react to posts. She describes her use as 'reading' and said, "I did not engage with it as far as making comments."

Jenn's OCoP engagement matches findings in related research. Participation levels primarily remain at consumption and lurking. This is consistent with Tseng and Kuo (2014) who find instructors in their study share in a limited manner but do so based on the development of high levels of self-efficacy. Data revealing increases in self-efficacy from this study, then, point to the notion that FAs involved in the OCoP for long periods of time might be more willing to share their technology integration knowledge with the whole community. After four semesters, however, Jenn is not at that stage.

Digital Pedagogy Orientation Levels and Influence of OCoP

Jenn is the only FA whose lesson analyses display a developmental pattern. Consequently, of the four FAs' lessons evaluated, Jenn was the most active in the OCoP. The pattern is not particularly strong but is traceable, showing growth in two of three constructs. Her pedagogical technology use and self-efficacy increase from the first lesson analysis to the fifth. In her interview responses, Jenn reports reading through OCoP content in both Canvas and Slack consistently each week. Canvas analytics support her description indicating she spends 1238 minutes or nearly 21 hours looking at and gaining information from the OCoP's Canvas component. Further, data show she reviewed 362 pages of content, which include repeated visits to some pages. Jenn similarly describes her Slack use. She says she reads through all posts, researches information based on content, and adds reactions to content she found useful. She refers to her weekly use by saying she dedicates "hours" to gathering knowledge from the OCoP.

Based on the data, Jenn engages with both digital spaces of the OCoP. She consumes and applies the shared content. Jenn also attends a synchronous professional learning session providing digital pedagogy strategies for peer reviews and peer critiques sessions in virtual learning environments. An additional synchronous session about active engagement with digital tools was offered, but Jenn could not attend due to a scheduling conflict. She accessed and viewed the recorded session, however.

Considering the results, then, attributing growth to active use of the OCoP may be a reasonable, albeit tentative conclusion. Reviewing Jenn's scores from the lesson analyses reveals she increases her pedagogical technology integration and related self-efficacy. The area in which she does not experience improvements is that of technology skills. Surveying the content emphasis in the OCoP potentially explains why Jenn may not exhibit a change in her technological skills, which includes her use of the LMS, creating professional digital content such as slide decks and videos, and integrating technology applications masterfully in her teaching sessions and shared resources. The OCoP does not include specific learning opportunities for this type of development. Instead, digital pedagogy experiences, theory, and tools dominate the content. Lacking are tutorials on digital content creation, organizing Canvas content, and basic technology use. Peeraer and Van Petegem (2012) identify facilitated and sustained OCoPs as a "best hope" (p. 1052) for professional learning experiences to expand teacher educators' knowledge and abilities. Jenn's active participation in the OCoP and evident gains from it support this notion.

LIMITATIONS

I am aware of and considered potential threats to validity, which are possible issues that can compromise data collection, data analysis, and conclusions researchers draw about data (Ivankova, 2015). Additionally, I am aware of and recognized potential limitations. To mitigate these threats and limitations, and to increase validity and trustworthiness, I identified the concerns and efforts to address them. Related to history and influences outside the intervention (Smith & Glass, 1987), I recognized knowledge may have come from PD sessions prior to joining the OCoP. Especially due to the switch to remote learning related to COVID-19, FAs had college-wide workshops available to them. Remote learning could have also resulted in maturation, internal unrelated growth (Smith & Glass, 1987), if FAs developed technology and skills from their intensive experiences through increased uses of digital technologies. Also, this study is contextually based and findings are not generalizable.

IMPLICATIONS FOR PRACTICE

An online community of practice is a potentially effective method of delivering professional learning, connecting instructors, sharing resources, and engaging faculty members. Results of the study indicate Jenn benefitted and perceived she learned and strengthened technology integration abilities due to the experiences. However, the number of FAs who engaged in the OCoP, attend live learning sessions, used professional learning resources, and spent productive time in the digital spaces was only a fraction of total FAs. In this study, about 33% of FAs used the OCoP with varied engagement levels. Considering nearly 38% of the fall 2020 semester's courses were taught by FAs, that engagement level does not ensure part-time faculty are capably delivering effective technology-infused instruction to teacher candidates (TCs) in the college.

Due to part-time status, most FAs are lurkers and passive consumers in the OCoP. Interview responses indicated that is due to a lack of self-efficacy or a perception of having limited or unimportant knowledge to share with the community. Efforts to bolster FAs' contributions would benefit all community members. Including them in more conversations about instruction and professional learning might encourage them to use the space more and add their ideas to it. A possible method for this could be inviting FAs to present short learning sessions or record videos describing teaching strategies through the OCoP. Thereafter, their contributions could become part of the curated resources in the space. This could affect their self-efficacy and perceptions that they have worthy knowledge to share. Building connections and community among all members could lead to more activity and use.

For a medium such as this to achieve full capacity and have the desired outcome of supporting part-time faculty members, other changes are necessary. First, promotion of the OCoP must be more widespread and frequent. I served as the main proponent of the OCoP even though the faculty professional development team knew it was the primary connection and communication source for FAs. On a very limited basis, those team members encouraged its use. Beyond their introduction of the OCoP during FA orientation at the start of the semester, I observed that only two members of that team engaged in the OCoP. That presence was restricted to the first week of the semester. Other faculty members and college leadership also did not actively promote it as an informational space for FAs. Without that promotion and direction, FAs are more apt to avoid it or use it on a limited basis.

Second, FAs should have pathways for learning and connection to all colleagues in teacher preparation programs. Membership of the OCoP included FAs and the faculty development team members. With a small number (five) of full-time faculty members included in the OCoP, FAs' networking and learning options are limited. Likewise, those five faculty members could not be responsible for facilitating the OCoP. A better structure would place all teacher preparation faculty, regardless of status, in the OCoP. With a completed adoption by college leadership, all FAs and full-time faculty members would have incentive to engage in networking and resource-sharing in the OCoP.

Third, if college leadership supports an organized effort to encourage and promote participation, engagement levels in the OCoP may increase. FAs are already less involved and less aware due to their part-time status and other obligations such as full-time employment elsewhere. For that reason, they may forget about the OCoP if they only hear about it at the start of their teaching terms. Specific outreach strategies, reminders, and other communication methods could consistently lead them to the OCoP as a place for help and learning options. Moreover, instructors are more likely to use the digital spaces if the OCoP is a centralized location consisting of all necessary resources and information. During the time of this study, the OCoP was just 'another' place for FAs to visit along with their email, the teacher preparation website, and content-specific online shared spaces. For more effective and continued use, the OCoP should have all instructional content and connections available for centralized and quick access. By promoting a clear pathway to the OCoP for digital pedagogy and technology integration learning, instructors will have less need to take separate paths to try to achieve similar outcomes.

Finally, content changes may also improve use of the OCoP and benefit participants. Based on the study's findings, Jenn, who was most active, did not experience gains with respect to her technology fluency due to a lack of specific learning options for functional technology skill development in the space. An aim of the OCoP should be to assist FAs with their growth in technology fluency or technology literacy as well as digital pedagogy. Surveying members about their needs would also influence available resources and learning opportunities. During the study, I sent announcements in Canvas and posted questions in Slack asking what FAs needed with respect to integrating technology into instruction, but I did not have any responses. A more structured survey, sent by college leadership or course coordinators to all members of the OCoP, would direct FAs to content in the OCoP, which could affect the levels of engagement. Developing the OCoP into an active space with coordinated methods for FAs to achieve educational technology growth will contribute to their transference to their students—future teachers who will daily be manipulating the 'middle conditions' through which they will guide their learners.

REFERENCES

Abbitt, J. T. (2011). An investigation of the relationship between self-efficacy beliefs about technology integration and technological pedagogical content knowledge (TPACK) among preservice teachers. *Journal of Digital Learning in Teacher Education, 27*(4), 134–143. https://doi.org/10.1080/21532974.2011.10784670

Bandura, A. (1977). *Social learning theory.* Prentice Hall.

Bandura, A. (1997). *Self-efficacy: The exercise of control.* Freeman.

Belland, B. R. (2009). Using the theory of habitus to move beyond the study of barriers to technology integration. *Computers & Education, 52*(2), 353–364. https://doi.org/10.1016/j.compedu.2008.09.004

Buss, R. R. (2018). Using action research as a signature pedagogy to develop EdD students' inquiry as practice skills. *Impacting Education: Journal on Transforming Professional Practice, 3*(1), 23–31. https://doi:10.5195/ie.2018.46

Buss, R. R., Foulger, T. S., Wetzel, K., & Lindsey, L. (2018). Preparing teachers to integrate technology into K–12 instruction II: Examining the effects of technology-infused methods courses and student teaching. *Journal of Digital Learning in Teacher Education, 34,* 134–150. doi: 10.1080/21532974.2018.1437852

Buss, R., Wetzel, K., Foulger, T. S., & Lindsey, L. (2015). Preparing teachers to integrate technology into K–12 instruction: Comparing a stand-alone course with a technology-infused approach. *Journal of Digital Learning in Teacher Education, 31,* 169–172. doi: 10.180/21532974.2015.1055012

Charmaz, K. (2014). *Constructing grounded theory.* Sage Publications, Inc.

Council for the Accreditation of Educator Preparation. (2013). *2013 CAEP Standards.* http://caepnet.org/standards/archive-standards/2013-itp/introduction

Council of Chief State School Officers. (2013). *Interstate Teacher Assessment and Support Consortium InTASC model core teaching standards and learning progressions for teachers 1.0: A resource for ongoing teacher development.* https://ccsso.org/resource-library/intasc-model-core-teaching-standards-and-learning-progressions-teachers-10

Creswell, J. W., & Creswell, J. D. (2018). *Research design: Qualitative, quantitative, and mixed methods approaches.* Sage Publications, Inc.

Dewey, J. (1916). *Democracy and education: An introduction to the philosophy of education.* The Free Press.

Dorner, H., & Kumar, S. (2016). Online collaborative mentoring for technology integration in pre-service teacher education. *TechTrends: Linking Research & Practice to Improve Learning, 60*(1), 48–55. https://doi.org/10.1007/s11528-015-0016-1

Foulger, T. S., Buss, R. R., Wetzel, K., & Lindsey, L. (2015). Instructors' growth in TPACK: Teaching technology-infused methods courses to preservice teachers. *Journal of Digital Learning in Teacher Education, 31*(4), 134–147. https://doi.org/10.1080/21532974.2015.1055010

Foulger, T. S., Graziano, K. J., Schmidt-Crawford, D., & Slykhuis, D. A. (2017). Teacher educator technology competencies. *Journal of Technology and Teacher Education, 25*(4), 413–448. https://www.learntechlib.org/p/181966/

Foulger, T. S., Wetzel, K., & Buss, R. R. (2019). Moving toward a technology infusion approach: Considerations for teacher preparation programs. *Journal of Digital Learning in Teacher Education, 35*(2), 79–91. https://doi.org/10.1080/21532974.2019.1568325

Glaser, B., & Strauss, A. (1967). *The discovery of grounded theory*. Aldine Publishing Co.

Greene, J. C. (2007). *Mixed methods in social inquiry*. Jossey-Bass.

International Society for Technology in Education. (2017). *ISTE standards for educators*. https://www.iste.org/standards/for-educators

Ivankova, N. V. (2015). *Mixed methods applications in action research: From methods to community action*. Sage Publications, Inc.

Karam, R., Straus, S. G., Byers, A., Kase, C. A., & Cefalu, M. (2018). The role of online communities of practice in promoting sociotechnical capital among science teachers. *Educational Technology Research and Development, 66*(2), 215–245. https://doi.org/10.1007/s11423-017-9541-2

Kolb, L. (2017). *Learning first, technology second: The educator's guide to designing authentic lessons*. International Society for Technology in Education.

Macià, M., & García, I. (2016). Informal online communities and networks as a source of teacher professional development: A review. *Teaching and Teacher Education, 55*, 291–307. https://doi.org/10.1016/j.tate.2016.01.021

Maxwell, J. A. (2013). *Qualitative research design: An interactive approach*. Sage Publications, Inc.

Mishra, P., & Koehler, M. J. (2006). Technological pedagogical content knowledge: A framework for teacher knowledge. *Teachers College Record, 108*(6), 1017–1054. https://doi.org/10.1111/j.1467-9620.2006.00684.x

Office of Educational Technology (OET). (2016). *Advancing educational technology in teacher preparation: Policy brief*. https://tech.ed.gov/teacherprep/

Peeraer, J., & Van Petegem, P. (2012). The limits of programmed professional development on integration of information and communication technology in education. *Australasian Journal of Educational Technology, 28*(6), 1039–1056. https://doi.org/10.14742/ajet.809

Saldaña, J. (2016). *The coding manual for qualitative researchers*. Sage Publications, Inc.

Schmidt, D. A., Baran, E., Thompson, A. D., Mishra, P., Koehler, M. J., & Shin, T. S. (2009). Technological pedagogical content knowledge (TPACK) the development and validation of an assessment instrument for preservice teachers. *Journal of Research on Technology in Education, 42*(2), 123–149. https://www.tandfonline.com/doi/abs/10.1080/15391523.2009.10782544

Smith, M. L., & Glass, G. V. (1987). Experimental studies. In M. L. Smith & G. V. Glass, *Research and evaluation in education and the social sciences*. Allyn and Bacon.

Smith, S. U., Hayes, S., & Shea, P. (2017). A critical review of the use of Wenger's community of practice (CoP) theoretical framework in online and blended learning research, 2000–2014. *Online Learning, 21*(1), 209–237. https://eric.ed.gov/?id=EJ1140262

Title 7, Education Chapter 2, State Board of Education, A.R.S. § 15-203(A)(1) (2018).

Tseng, F.-C., & Kuo, F.-Y. (2014). A study of social participation and knowledge sharing in the teachers' online professional community of practice. *Computers & Education, 72*, 37–47. https://doi.org/10.1016/j.compedu.2013.10.005

Wenger, E. (1998). *Communities of practice: Learning, meaning, and identity*. Cambridge University Press.

Wenger, E., White, N., & Smith, J. D. (2009). *Digital habitats: Stewarding technology for communities*. CPsquare.

Wengerishra, P., & Koehler, M. J. (2006). Technological pedagogical content knowledge: A framework for teacher knowledge. *Teachers College Record*, *108*(6), 1017–1054. http://citeseerx.ist.psu.edu/viewdoc/download?doi=10.1.1.523.3855&rep=rep1&type=pdf

Wetzel, K., Buss, R., Foulger, T. S., & Lindsey, L. (2014). Infusing educational technology in teaching methods courses: Successes and dilemmas. *Journal of Digital Learning in Teacher Education*, *30*(3), 89–103. https://doi.org/10.1080/21532974.2014.891877

CHAPTER 4

CLOSING THE FEEDBACK LOOP ON RUBRICS

From Design to Grading and Faculty Engagement

Melanie Kasparian and Mamta Saxena

INTRODUCTION

Transparent and intentional assessment design is essential to make concrete connections for students between learning outcomes and expected quality of work. Crafting quality and consistent rubrics for assessment and program evaluation is often done with assessment professionals in silos, but it cannot be completed without partnerships with faculty. There are also competing dialogues and tensions around the use of standard rubrics, academic freedom, and implications for policy and practice (McKnight et al., 2020). Rubrics can be used as effective tools for learning, teaching, grading, and reliable assessment data sources, but only with faculty collaboration and acknowledgment of some inherent pedagogical challenges and shortcomings.

Research suggests that including rubrics in courses enhances instruction. Jonsson and Svingby (2007) surveyed 75 studies relevant to the reliability and effectiveness of rubrics. They concluded that quality rubrics can increase the accuracy of performance assessment scoring and when complemented with other integrat-

---

Faculty Development: Achieving Change Through Action Research, pages 45–59.
Copyright © 2024 by Information Age Publishing
www.infoagepub.com
All rights of reproduction in any form reserved.

ed assessment tools, improve the reliability. Rubrics are excellent substitutes for traditional testing methods that assess the ability to memorize information, not conceptual understanding (Montgomery, 2000). Rubrics can promote learning and improve instruction by making expectations and criteria explicit. However, just like any assessment effort, implementing consistent use of rubrics requires faculty collaboration.

This study was conducted by the Academic Quality and Assessment (AQA) unit at a nonprofit university. This study combines action learning and action research to better understand elements of assessment practices and that of the faculty to answer the question: How can we increase faculty engagement in the use of analytic rubrics to facilitate transparent assessment design? This study shares insights from the action research conducted to engage faculty in the design and consistent implementation of rubrics. It aims to discuss strategies of faculty and learner empowerment through successes and the failed efforts when assessment is tied solely with the program evaluation process.

BACKGROUND AND CONTEXT

Conflicting Assessment Paradigms

One of the major findings of the national survey on student learning outcomes was that "faculty are the key to moving assessment forward" (NILOA, 2014). Beyond buy-in, faculty needs to be involved in any implementation effort from start to finish as "the real promise of assessment depends on significantly growing and deepening faculty involvement" (Hutchings, 2010, p. 6). The primary challenge in building trust with faculty is to help them view assessment as a driver for improving the curriculum and the teaching-learning practice ("assessment for improvement"), not just reporting for accreditation purposes ("assessment for accountability").

Assessment professionals and organizations invest a lot of energy and enthusiasm in promoting assessment to faculty as a vehicle for improving learning. The debate on whether assessment for accountability and assessment for improvement can coexist or if one can complement another has been ongoing (Banta, 2007). The assessment community has long tried to convince faculty and institutions that the primary purpose of assessment is improvement, even if the same assessment process could be used to address accountability for accreditation purposes. Ewell (2009) accurately cautions that the adoption of either one of the two perspectives will dictate the institutional approach and efforts around assessment (what to assess, how to assess, and for whom), which in turn has a direct impact on faculty buy-in and support. The initial challenge with rubrics is to address the accountability-improvement tension for faculty. While assessment in higher education may not be able to fully resolve this debate, we tried to address the tension by becoming more transparent about communicating the results of using rubrics with the faculty and leadership.

Ewell (2009) offers some guiding principles to respond to external accountability while preserving the institutional need for continuous improvement. The first step is to change the assessment narrative for faculty and leaders from a compliance exercise to assessment for collective responsibility of teaching and learning so faculty and institutions are accountable to themselves and to their students. Another critical step for assessment-based improvement to be transparent is that learning outcomes must be present and aligned in catalogs, syllabi, assignment descriptions, and the criteria used for grading within the rubrics. Most importantly, the improvement goals tied to the learning outcomes and rubrics data, must be "continuously mapped and reinforced by the teaching-learning process" across the curriculum as part of a systemic assessment cycle (p. 19).

Competing Dialogues and Tensions around Rubrics

One of the rationales behind expanding the use of analytics rubrics is to help achieve uniformity regarding grading practices across courses. The most conventional concern among faculty has been about the standardization of rubrics. McKnight et al. (2020) discuss competing arguments around the use of a compulsory rubric at their university with the premise that assessment choice is always grounded in pedagogy that speaks of epistemologies, ideology, and power positions at institutions. The arguments relate to how a compulsory rubric can pose obstacles in educating twenty-first-century learners, designing authentic assessment, embedding indigenous approaches, inviting diverse perspectives, and honoring academic freedom. The authors acknowledge that the competing discourse is a starting point in recognizing the frustrations and tensions between the "academic and administration" or "student and assessor" along with an opportunity to collectively explore diversity in assessment needs to strive for quality in education.

Challenges with Annual Assessment

Typical summative assessment relies on collecting data annually for culminating demonstration of competencies, usually in the capstone courses in the program. Of more significance is real-time assessment that drive curriculum changes to address teaching and learning issues advantageous for currently enrolled students. Thus, working with programs to offer reporting by term that was easily accessible proved to be a more effective strategy for identifying needed curriculum changes and supporting struggling students for visible improvement efforts.

Maki (2017) proposed six guiding principles of real-time student assessment: (a) needs to be internally driven and motivated and part of institutional mission and shared commitment, not a response to external accountability; (b) requires inclusive commitment and engagement of internal stakeholders from leaders to system administrators, full-time and part-time faculty, institution experts, and enrolled students; (c) must have extensive collaboration across the institution to leverage expertise and processes for data collection, analysis, reporting, and acting upon the findings (institutional research, registrar, student information system, technology services, advising, student affairs); (d) depends on continuous tracking, analysis and reporting of assessment results through a systemic assessment cycle with appropriate tools; (e) includes disaggregating assessment results based on demographics and responding to the academic challenges and struggles related to underperformance, especially for the marginalized students; and (f) must be valued by the institution to commit to dedicated resources and time.

METHODS

One college at a nonprofit university located in New England was the site for the study. The college has over 35 academic programs and enrolls over 9,000 students yearly. For this study, we combined action learning and action research to increase faculty engagement in the use of rubrics. What is embedded in the iterative, cyclical assessment process is action learning, which is grounded in a concept of "L=P+Q, where learning equals programmed knowledge plus questioning insight" when a small group of individuals work together to solve their problems and implement solutions (Sankaran, 2015, p. 49). Sankaran explains the synergy between action learning and action research and the usefulness of combining the two to solve real problems and produce actionable and rigorous outcomes (2015).

Participants

The participants for both Cycle 1 and Cycle 2 were full-time faculty leads for each academic program, both graduate and undergraduate programs from a variety of academic subject areas. In total there were 25 participants, as some faculty leads oversee multiple academic programs.

Data Collection

This study utilized the annual program reporting process to reflect upon the experiences of using analytic rubrics with faculty. The collective reflection included discussion on the rubric design, connections with program learning outcomes (PLOs) and assignment descriptions, reporting, and implementation challenges. This study occurred over several years of reporting—from 2017 to 2021.

For cycle 1, the unit held one-on-one monthly consultations with lead faculty via semi-structured meetings that lasted from 30–90 minutes including conversations on effective practices, success stories, and opportunities for improvement. We engaged in insightful questioning to help discover solutions for making the analytic rubrics more robust by establishing clear connections with PLOs, competencies, activities, and formative assessments. Cycle 2 had the same treatment with semi-structured monthly meetings with lead faculty. Our unit and faculty were essentially "learning from concrete experience and critical reflection on the experience through group discussion, trial and error, discovery and learning from each other" (Zuber-

Skerritt, 2002, p. 114). In this study, faculty became co-researchers and not informants with a shared purpose of making measurable and noticeable improvements.

Data Analysis

Data analysis from both cycles were drawn from three areas: (1) rubrics implementation rates by program; (2) rubrics implementation and value proposition challenges based on themes from annual reports; and (3) meaningful use of rubrics and data conversations, based on the collective reflection of faculty leads.

First, we applied quantitative metrics on the use of rubrics for assessment data collection on PLOs. Results were tracked as the percent of programs that implemented rubrics, using data from the learning management system (LMS). Sample data from 2018 through 2019 showed that % of course sections with rubrics data was on the rise from 24 to 28 percent.

Second, we identified common themes from programs' annual evaluation reports (continuous improvement goals). Extrapolating from the themes from annual reports in Cycle 1, we adopted several changes in our process for Cycle 2. We partnered with faculty and created assignment templates to make rubrics transparent and applied embedded assessment strategies. We also created a rubrics repository that hosted a plethora of sample rubrics based on assignment type and skills-based rubrics adapted from American Association of Colleges and Universities' VALUE Rubrics (Rhodes, 2010). Through meaningful conversation about the role of rubrics, making data accessible, and data visualization techniques (see Table 4.1 and Figure 4.1), we were able to make the results explicit for faculty. The rubric results below from a sample assignment are presented in two ways: summary statistics and stacked bar charts, which indicate that learners performed best on "describing the problems" and worst on "concept clarity." This level of data was useful to flag courses and assessments and take appropriate action and prompted lead faculty to revisit results across sections to see variability across instructors, level of clarity in the task or assignment description and rubric descriptors, and formative activities to check for scaffolding.

TABLE 4.1. Summary Statistics on Rubric Results from a Data Visualization Assignment

Rubric Criteria	Count	Average	Median	Mode	Standard Deviation
Description of the problem	139	3.29	3	3	0.71
Choice of visualization	140	3.19	3	3	0.77
Approach to solving the problem	140	3.05	3	3	0.74
Concept clarity	59	2.83	3	3	0.75
Quality of the contribution	81	3.12	3	3	0.66
Writing	140	3.24	3	3	0.66

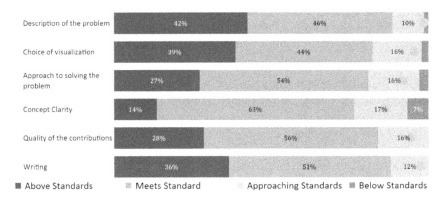

FIGURE 4.1. Rubric Results from a Data Visualization Assignment, Percent of Learners for each Level of Achievement

Finally, and most impactful, was the collective reflection in the one-on-one monthly consultations with faculty. Cycle 1 analysis and findings were primarily focused on spreading the word about rubrics, training faculty on the use of rubrics, and quantifying the effort. Cycle 2 analysis is more qualitative in nature and indicate a deeper engagement and development of a culture of inquiry among faculty, as well as the quality of rubrics. Faculty became curious about how rubrics can promote thinking for students and if they truly contribute to the improvement of the teaching-learning practice. For cycle 2, we focused on changing the narrative, further collaboration, and refining practices related to rubric use and reporting.

Changing the Narrative: Improvement, Internal Drive, and Shared Commitment

In Cycle 2, we incorporated Maki's (2017) six guiding principles described in the *Background and Context* section in several ways. We co-lead rubrics projects such as rubrics design, norming, onboarding, training, analysis for special courses (experiential, remedial, or entry-level) as a response to faculty's interest and curiosity. This created a sense of internal ownership, inclusive commitment, and engagement in enhancing the rubrics. We also worked with programs to identify other courses at the beginning or middle of the program that were meaningful to their program goals. We worked with the college deans and senior leadership to acquire the needed resources, tools, and host training sessions to share findings.

Extensive Collaboration for Real-Time and Disaggregated Data

In Cycle 1, aggregate findings were shared in the annual report for each program with the expectation that faculty will reflect and write a narrative independently. We changed this practice in Cycle 2 to adopt an approach proposed by

Ewell (2009): collectively look at the disaggregated results for specific populations or outcomes dimensions to discuss what the data means and its implications for action. This process raised faculty curiosity and led to more questions and demand for further analysis. The new approach proved to be far more effective in engaging faculty in the assessment conversation in a meaningful way for real change, rather than just sharing a "data dump" of aggregate results. Moreover, this approach led to a positive impact on teaching-learning practices and helped refine college-level policies and practices.

We partnered with teams across the university to invest in real-time assessment resources, processes, and platforms to create reports, visualization, and self-serving dashboards where data was continually updated. We were able to offer assessment data that could be disaggregated by term and student demographics. Figure 3 showcases an interactive dashboard that allows faculty to filter their assessment data by different parameters. We allocated sessions for faculty to come together to discuss data that would yield more actionable findings.

As identified in Cycle 1, reporting and interpreting results is essential to make the connection with program changes and yearly goals to make a case for improvement efforts.

Refining Practice: Rubrics Norming, Math, and Consistency

Serving as facilitators to the conversations, we hosted data and rubric norming sessions with multiple faculty teaching the same course. With regards to rubrics, many were too summative in nature and had criteria that were not specifically relevant or were being deployed inconsistently. Schoepp, Danaher and Kranov (2018) stress that "rubric norming sessions are necessary to gain a shared under-

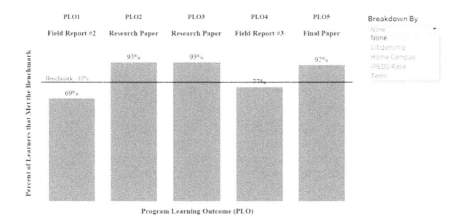

FIGURE 4.2. Sample Assessment Results of Percent of Learners that Met the Benchmark

standing of the rubric criteria employed and of performance standards and thresholds." (p.2). We worked with faculty to customize the generic skills-based rubrics adopted from the repository of rubrics to make stronger connections with task descriptions. In addition, we needed to shift from rubrics for grading to rubrics for assessing as part of the program reporting process. Goggins (2013) discusses the challenge of converting a rubric score on an assignment to a letter grade. Seemingly easy in terms of computations, but difficult for interpretation. The author stresses the importance of describing how a rubric is scored to learners so that it is easy to interpret. Similarly, the design of the rubric criteria needs to be specific enough to the assignment, yet broad enough to be used for summative assessment. These rubric norming conversations with faculty were filled with deep and meaningful conversations about grading scales, the number of criteria within the rubric, and how specific the rubric descriptors should be.

Transparency and communication across the college were essential for consistency of implementation. The college established a Principal Instructor (PI) model where the PI serves as mentors to the part-time faculty teaching in the various course sections and as advisors to respective faculty leads. They focus on curriculum design, development, assessment implementation, learning analytics data review, and section instructors' onboarding and training. Select programs leveraged features within the LMS to share signature assignments and rubrics more easily.

Trustworthiness and Quality Assurance

Several methods were deployed to maintain data integrity. The participants as lead faculty were from different programs of study and themes identified spanned across various academic disciplines. As part of the annual reporting process, all narratives and goals were documented in archived reports over the course of several years. We took copious notes as well in the consultations and were able to triangulate the meeting notes with report narratives. Faculty debriefs on the themes every year were conducted to ensure equivalence between our interpretations and faculty perspectives.

Findings

In terms of implementation, the percent of programs implementing rubrics within the learning management system for continuous improvement and program evaluation increased. The most common rubrics across the college were discussions and assignments. The most common criteria (rows of the rubric) were writing and analysis. Skills such as critical thinking, connection, research, and presentation were also prevalent.

Examining the themes from the programs for Cycle 1 (2017, 2018, and 2019), the most common goals faculty drafted were related to the consistency of implementation of the rubrics. Faculty leads defined assessment plans and rubrics but fell short of consistent implementation within the program repeatedly. This made data collection and reporting difficult as we could not aggregate and report on all sections of a course. Data was not disaggregated in a way that was meaningful for faculty. Based upon the collaborative reflection with faculty on actions taken in Cycle 1, we recognized the following issues:

- Faculty still associated the rubrics work primarily with annual reporting and no correlation with curriculum improvement.
- Faculty found it difficult to make meaningful connections with real action when looking at the aggregate data.
- Faculty were not convinced that data on only upper-level courses or capstone would offer a holistic picture of the student learning experience.
- Based on the size of the program and the number of full-time faculty, programs faced challenges in consistent implementation due to limited time and resources for monitoring or training part-time faculty.

After Cycle 2, rubric data was shared in a dashboard, with the new capability to disaggregate by term, program and student attributes. As a result, the analysis, reflection, and actions became much more robust and widespread. More profound was the faculty feedback on the relevancy and use of rubrics for their teaching practices, along with constructive critique and some pedagogical dilemmas and concerns around the standardization of rubrics across sections. Below are some insights based upon the collaborative reflection from faculty leads and cohorts of faculty across programs related to rubrics:

- Faculty valued the process of designing analytic rubrics for a given task as it prompted them to unpack the learning from a student's perspective, outcomes from a content perspective, and required scaffolding via formative activities.
- Faculty appreciated the use of rubrics for adding efficiency when dealing with large sections. Also, it helped them respond to student inquiries when grades were in question by pointing to the explicit criteria and connection with the task description.
- One of the pedagogical concerns related to rubrics is the reductionist approach where faculty are asked to simplify complex tasks or skills descriptions to fit the rubric criteria. Rubric design felt like boxing learning in a matrix with a focus on quantifying performance for data collection and grading purposes. For comprehensive summative assessments, it was difficult to craft criteria that would be explicit enough to help students fully grasp the depth and breadth of the task or expectations.
- Some faculty expressed concerns about the mechanical use of rubrics primarily as a grading tool with little value in teaching-learning or curriculum enhancement. The same is true for students who use it as an instrument to get good grades and precisely match the creator's expectations, which may limit deeper learning.

- Some faculty identified the lack of rubrics training for part-time faculty as a factor for bad practices in rubrics design and use where feedback for criteria is vague and the math unclear for students.
- The involvement of students in the design or review of rubrics was expressed both as an opportunity and a concern. For equitable practices, including students' voices, their frame of reference and context, and having them use rubrics as a self-assessment tool was deemed critical.
- One other concern was the standardization of rubrics across sections and the question of academic freedom.

DISCUSSION

Research and literature on rubrics present several benefits of using rubrics such as increasing transparency for assessment criteria, promoting thinking and learning, and improving learning outcomes and the assessment cycle (Andrade, 2000; Jonsson, 2014; Miknis et al., 2020). Concurrently, the literature abounds in highlighting the problematic nature of rubrics. We list here some of the themes found in the literature that align with what we discovered in Cycle 2 results, based on faculty feedback and testimonials.

Faculty's Perception of Rubrics

While Jonsson (2014) asserts that rubrics are excellent tools for providing transparency in assessment, Bearman and Ajjawi label transparency as a metaphor that seems to create a perception of fairness and consistency when "transparent assessment criteria are surprisingly problematic" (p. 359). The authors further explain that efforts to be completely explicit result in over-specification or mechanistic instructions especially with complex, authentic assessments and it becomes challenging for faculty to articulate and for students to understand the expectations. This poses barriers to a holistic and deeper understanding of both the content and what constitutes quality. Moreover, students may view transparency as a tool for gaming the system and meeting the minimal expectation specified in the rubrics to attain A grades (2021). Faculty find it impossible to pack the expectations for complex masters or doctoral level summative tasks in a single rubric.

Use of Rubrics as Teaching, Learning, and Grading Tools

Andrade claims that rubrics are "teaching tools that support learning and development of sophisticated thinking skills" (2000, p. 13). Kohn challenges this notion in that if the goal of authentic assessment is to find alternatives to grades, rubrics are only a novel way of legitimizing grades that have negative effects on students based on research as "they tend to think less deeply, avoid taking risks and lose interest in the learning itself" (2006, p. 12). Maja (2006) defies the use of rubrics and argues against boxing the messy process of learning and assessment to a few rows and columns that minimizes the complexity of the content, the skills, and the expectations. Such concerns are especially specific to the masters and doctoral level programs, based on feedback from some faculty. The primary concern is that the use of rubrics to assign a grade to a summative assessment may serve the reporting needs, but it fails to represent the expected depth of learning and the value of rich formative feedback provided to students throughout the course.

Another problematic assumption is that rubrics are grading tools to help assess student work faster and to justify grades (Andrade, 2000). Rubrics cannot be used as a substitute for detailed and targeted feedback that helps guide the learners in addressing the gaps in their learning. Andrade clarified that a good rubric offers "individualized and constructive critique in a manageable timeframe" but it does not replace the time spent in providing his students written and verbal feedback (2005, p. 29). Cockeet and Jackson (2018) caution that rubrics cannot address all issues related to feedback: quality, usefulness, and consistency. Therefore, we need to look at the research literature that offers unique perspectives and approaches when using rubrics so they can truly serve as teaching and learning tools as opposed to completely abandoning them as imperfect grading tools. Our unit does not prescribe compulsory rubrics for programs but works collaboratively with faculty in each program to help craft rubrics for summative assignments where we collect PLO data with a shared understanding from other faculty in the program.

Nonetheless, there are some lessons learned from this discussion. We can work on the collegial acknowledgment of the struggles of faculty with the use of rubrics (pedagogical, administrative, others) and engage in a constructive dialogue around how to address accountability while respecting diversity, context, and academic freedom. We can use the diverse experiences and expertise of faculty to explore other alternative methods of assessment to build a diverse portfolio of assessment tools, while sustaining the uniformity for quality learner experience.

Perspectives on Effective and Innovative Practices

A foremost aspect when designing rubrics is to engage students in the development of a rubric. To be most effective as a learning tool, faculty must: design tasks for students to help them understand the purpose and criteria of assessment; share examples of high- and low-quality work; give opportunities for self and peer evaluation of their work based on the rubric; and allow students to submit multiple drafts based on feedback (Goodrich, 1997; O'Halloran & O'Halloran, 2001; Andrage; 2000; Norton, 2004). Miknis, Davies, and Johnson (2020) explored the benefits of rubrics in improving learner outcomes using self-assessment rubrics. The findings demonstrated that it helped students become more self-regulating and self-aware of their strengths and weaknesses and helped assessors in revising the curriculum to facilitate improved learning outcomes.

Experts caution that the standards of validity, reliability, and equity apply to rubrics too. They must be designed with acceptable standards, aligned with the curriculum, and be able to pass the test of consistency and accuracy when used by different people. Gender, race, ethnicity, or class must be factored in to check for equity issues. (Andrade, 2005; Moskal & Leydens, 2000; Payne, 2003).

Bearman and Ajjawi (2021) propose a new way of conceptualizing assessment criteria as 'invitational enactments' by inviting students into a 'productive space.' The authors provide concrete examples of how to do this. One should avoid highly directive prescriptive ("include five citations") or too abstract criteria ("writing is coherent") to enable meaningful enactment of the criteria. The materials design should consider the context of the student (level, social, material) and offer opportunities for students to share their thinking on the task and the criteria. If using generic rubrics, one must consider the context of the student in the task descriptions, exemplars, clear explanations, and descriptors of quality expectations to inform action. Faculty must offer students multiple opportunities to make sense of the quality indicators in the criterion across multiple tasks and assignments for sustained learning. Most importantly, inviting students to interrogate what they think the rubric is inviting them to do where they can articulate why and how their work has met the criteria and how the assessment materials inform their thinking and work. This approach could address some of the concerns about including student voice and context into rubrics.

Howell's (2014) multivariate, quasi-experimental study on the impact of grading rubric use on academic outcomes affirms that rubrics have a positive impact on academic outcomes but also cautions that rubrics are "not a "silver bullet" solution for bolstering academic performance among undergraduates" (p. 406). Most importantly, the bad practices of using rubrics may cause harm to student learning. This underscores the importance of appropriate training and support for faculty on the use of rubrics so they can maximize the use for promoting thinking and learning and incorporate them as grading tools that assist with achieving consistency and accountability.

Limitations

Critics have highlighted several limitations of action research relative to experimental research such as clear distinction between action and research, a lack of external validity, rigor, and objectivity. Kock (2004) lists three threats to action research: uncontrollability (lack of control over the environment under study), contingency (lack of generalizability), and subjectivity (researcher's bias) that may lead to negative research consequences. There are similar limitations worth noting in our research.

While the AQA team researched and worked with programs over a period of several years, societal and college-wide changes impacted the research, such as faculty turnover, changes to policy and processes, and college's strategic priorities. Faculty involved in this study were partners in the research and actively participated in the assessment process, resulting in selection bias. Furthermore, differences exist in assessment practices across institutions, and the perceptions of the faculty in this study might vary from faculty in other institutions. The themes included in the findings might not fully translate to other institutions. In addition, data on rubric implementation does not speak to use of quality rubrics. Student voices, one of the key stakeholders, were not part of the study and is an area of further research.

IMPLICATIONS

According to Hanover Research (2020), institutions are moving away from investing in assessment for solely accreditation and other compliance requirements and are more committed to improving student learning outcomes. While the focus of this study is specific to rubrics, the debate on assessment for accountability versus assessment for improvement is ongoing and is an area of future research. Regarding faculty collaboration, McConnell (2012) shares examples from institutional and state-wide collaborations on rubrics and asserts that they could be powerful tools for promoting and facilitating collaboration between faculty and assessment professionals. The AQA unit is committed to investing in assessment resources and training for faculty and establishing trust and partnerships.

Future research should address the following: (a) how do institutions create spaces for constructive critique of assessment practices to acknowledge the tensions and frustrations of faculty; (b) how to address the issue of power and agency and bring faculty voices in the exploration of alternative assessment tools for positive outcomes; (c) how to improve reporting on assessment data that is most meaningful for faculty and in-real time; and (d) how to implement inclusive practices that help address inequities and include student voices and context in the assessment process such as writing learning outcomes, assignment or rubrics design, or use of assessment data.

REFERENCES

Andrade, H. G. (2000). Using rubrics to promote thinking and learning. *Educational Leadership, 57*(5), 13–18.

Andrade, H. G. (2005). Teaching with rubrics: The good, the bad, and the ugly. *College Teaching, 53*(1), 27–31.

Association of American Colleges and Universities. (2014). *Degree Qualification Profile*. Retrieved on November 28, 2021 from https://www.aacu.org/degree-qualifications-profile

Banta, T. W. (2007). Can assessment for accountability complement assessment for improvement? *Peer Review, 9*(2), 9–12.

Bearman, M., & Ajjawi, R. (2021). Can a rubric do more than be transparent? Invitation as a new metaphor for assessment criteria. *Studies in Higher Education, 46*(2), 359–368.

Cockett, A., & Jackson, C. (2018). The use of assessment rubrics to enhance feedback in higher education: An integrative literature review. *Nurse Education Today, 69*(2), 8–13.

Dick, B. (2001). Action research: Action and research. In S. Sankaran, B. Dick, R. Passfield, & P. Swepson (Eds.), *Effective change management using action learning and action research: Concepts, frameworks, processes and applications* (pp. 21–27). Southern Cross University Press.

Ewell, P. T. (2009, November). *Assessment, accountability, and improvement: Revisiting the tension.* (Occasional Paper No. 1). University of Illinois and Indiana University, National Institute for Learning Outcomes Assessment (NILOA).

Goggins Selke, M. (2013). *Rubric assessment goes to college: Objective, comprehensive evaluation of student work.* Rowman & Littlefield.

Goodrich, H. (1997). Understanding rubrics. *Educational Leadership, 54*(4), 14–17.

Guy, B., Feldman, T., Cain, C., Leesman, L., & Hood, C. (2020). Defining and navigating 'action' in a participatory action research project. *Educational Action Research, 28*(1), 142–153.

Hanover Research. (2020). *Best practices in learning outcomes assessment.* ETS Research Report Series.

Howell, R. J. (2014). Grading rubrics: hoopla or help? *Innovations in Education and Teaching International, 51*(4), 400–410.

Hutchings, P. (2010). *Opening doors to faculty involvement in assessment.* http://www.learningoutcomeassessment.org/documents/PatHutchings.pdf

Jonsson, A., & Svingby, G. (2007). The use of scoring rubrics. Reliability, validity, and educational consequences. *Educational Research Review 2*, 130–144.

Kock, N. (2004). The three threats of action research: A discussion of methodological antidotes in the context of an information systems study. *Decision Support Systems, 37*(2), 265–286.

Kohn, A. (2006). The trouble with rubrics. *English Journal, 95*(4), 12–15.

Kuh, G. D. (2007). Risky business: Promises and pitfalls of institutional transparency. *Change, 39*(5), 30–35.

Kuh, G. D., Jankowski, N., Ikenberry, S. O., & Kinzie, J. (2014). *Knowing what students know and can do: The current state of student learning outcomes assessment in US colleges and universities.* University of Illinois and Indiana University, National Institute for Learning Outcomes Assessment (NILOA).

Maki, P. L. (2017). *Real-time student assessment: Meeting the imperative for improved time to degree, closing the opportunity gap, and assuring student competencies for 21st century.* Stylus.

McConnell, K. D. (2012). Rubrics as catalyst for collaboration: A modest proposal. *European Journal of Higher Education, 3*(1), 74–88.

McKnight, L., Bennett, S., & Webster, S. (2020). Quality and tyranny: competing discourses around a compulsory rubric. *Assessment & Evaluation in Higher Education, 45*(8), 1192–1204.

Miknis, M., Davies, R., & Johnson, C. S. (2020). Using rubrics to improve the assessment lifecycle: A case study. *Higher Education Pedagogies, 5*(10), 200–209.

Montgomery, K. (2000). Classroom rubrics: Systematizing what teachers do naturally. *A Journal of Educational Strategies, Issues, and Ideas, 76*(3), 324–328.

Moskal, B., & Leydens, J. (2000). Scoring rubric development: Validity and reliability. *Practical Assessment, Research and Evaluation, 7*(10). http://PAREonline.net/getvn.aspv=7&n=10.

Norton, L. (2004). Using assessment criteria as learning criteria: A case study in psychology. *Assessment & Evaluation in Higher Education, 29*(6), 687–702.

O'Halloran, C. S., & O'Halloran, R. M. (2001). Recommending as teaching and learning tools. *Journal of Hospitality & Tourism Education, 13*(2), 56–59.

Payne, D. A. (2003). *Applied educational assessment.* (2nd ed.). Wadsworth/Thomson Learning.

Rhodes, T. (2010). *Assessing outcomes and improving achievement: Tips and tools for using rubrics.* Association of American Colleges and Universities.

Sankaran, S. (2015). Achieving synergy through combining action learning and action research. In J. Kearney & M. Todhunter (Eds.), *Lifelong action learning and research* (pp. 45–63). The Netherlands: Brill Sense.

Sankaran, S., & Dick, B. (2015). Linking theory and practice in using action-oriented methods. In B. Pasian (Ed.), *Designs, methods and practices for research of project management* (pp. 211–224). Gower.

Schoepp, K., Danaher, M., & Ater Kranov, A. (2018). An effective rubric norming process. *Practical Assessment, Research, and Evaluation, 23*(11), 2–6.

Wilkerson, J. R. (2020). Rubrics meeting quality assurance and improvement needs in the context of accreditation. *Quality Assurance in Education, 28*(1), 19-32.

Wilson, M. (2006). *Rethinking rubrics in writing assessment.* Heinemann.

Zuber-Skerritt, O. (2002). A model for designing action learning and action research programs. *The Learning Organization, 9*(4), 143–149.

CHAPTER 5

ENHANCING CLINICAL EXPERIENCES THROUGH ACTION RESEARCH

Teacher Educators Bridging the Gap Between Coursework and Field Experiences

Bjorg LeSueur, Tanya Pinkerton, and Andrea Weinberg

INTRODUCTION

Early childhood education (ECE) results in life-long benefits for children (e.g., Wylie & Vaughn, 2019) and is vital to a robust and thriving society (UNESCO, 2020). High quality teachers in ECE environments have knowledge of child development and developmentally appropriate practice, observe and document progress, embrace culturally and linguistically appropriate teaching practices, and use research-based approaches to support learning and development (NAEYC, 2019). It is imperative that preservice teachers (PST) gain not only theoretical knowledge in coursework but have opportunities to bridge theory and practice in clinical experiences (i.e., internships, student teaching) which occur in real-world classrooms. However, clinical experiences have been referred to as the "Achilles

---

Faculty Development: Achieving Change Through Action Research, pages 61–75.

heel" of teacher education (Darling-Hammond, 2009) because of the persistent challenge of bridging theory and practice. This action research (AR) study is focused on the engagement of stakeholders in a university-based teacher education program and local Head Start program to identify mechanisms for meaningful collaboration to design and implement clinical experiences with enhanced outcomes for PSTs and teachers alike. This chapter will illustrate the role of AR in critically evaluating the needs of a variety of stakeholders and using an iterative approach to implementing and reflecting on innovations for change.

BACKGROUND

Teachers represent the most influential school-based contribution to children's success (Chetty et al, 2014). High quality teachers are imperative; an integral aspect to a quality ECE workforce is rigorous teacher education. While early childhood educators in K–3 (and some preschool) classrooms must complete a Bachelor's degree and obtain state educator certification, there are no unified expectations for the education of those working with children before the age of five. There are numerous pathways to becoming a teacher in ECE classrooms, including four-year Bachelor's degree programs, two-year Associate's programs, non-degree certification programs, or even just a high school diploma or the equivalent. Credentialing and licensing criteria for birth to 5 educators vary across states (IMNRC, 2015). To briefly explain, outside of a few unique settings (e.g., district-based Developmental Preschool), in the state of Arizona where this study took place, the requirements to be a lead teacher in an early childhood setting from birth to age 5 not yet in kindergarten are a high school diploma, no criminal record, and yearly 18 hours of training each year the individual is employed. Those requirements are set by the department of health services which oversees licensing of childcare settings. A consequence of this lack of a standard qualification is fragmented and inconsistent program offerings at institutions of higher education. There are efforts to encourage Bachelor's degrees, including for Head Start programs, where 50% of teachers nationwide are to hold a Bachelor's degree in ECE or a related field (Head Start, 2013). Head start requires lead teachers to have completed a Child Development Associate Certificate and are working towards degree completion. While these efforts are slowly gaining traction (e.g., 72% of HS teachers have bachelor's; Head Start, 2013), because this particular metric for Head Start is at the national level, dramatic discrepancies in the education level of teachers exist across regions and sites. This fragmentation translates to an array of program offerings at institutes of higher education for aspiring early childhood educators that often lack continuity.

Early childhood educators should have a strong background in educational theory and child development. From birth to age 8, children experience a remarkable range of developmental stages and educational settings; therefore, education programs for ECE should provide varied opportunities for clinical experiences across early childhood settings inclusive of birth to grade 3 (age 8; INMRC,

2015). In teacher education programs, this means PSTs must split their clinical experiences between school-age classrooms (i.e., K–3) as well as birth to age 5 settings. The discrepancies in the qualifications and licensure requirements for early childhood educators present unique challenges for teacher educators. Specifically, the educational backgrounds of early childhood school-based teacher educators (e.g. mentor teachers) at clinical sites may be misaligned with the education requirements for licensure in early childhood (i.e., birth to 5 years) settings and the degree programs of the PSTs' they mentor. Though most educators in early childhood settings serving children birth to age 5 have not had the experience of completing a pre-service program, they are asked to play a pivotal role in supporting the development of teacher candidates during internships or student teaching placements—clinical experiences that they themselves did not have if they did not complete a teacher education program. What this means is, for example, a school-based teacher educator may not *have* the theoretical knowledge PSTs are introduced to in coursework because they themselves have not completed a degree program. Yet, bridging coursework and clinical experience is central to PSTs' path toward becoming a highly qualified teacher, and mentor teachers are tasked with supporting this. Therefore, creating a unique challenge for mentor teacher, and to teacher education broadly, where there may be a disconnect between what the PSTs are learning or asked to do in coursework (theory) and seeing and learning from mentors in practice.

Clinical Practice in Teacher Education

The responsibilities of school-based teacher educators within teacher education programs have increased in recent decades, with programmatic shifts many teacher education programs that emphasize clinical experiences and therefore rely more heavily on mentor teachers to support PST development (Cope & Stephen, 2001; NAEYC, 2019). This increased responsibility calls for shared understandings around the aims of the clinical experiences and support for developing the skills required for mentoring PSTs. Unfortunately, however, it is "widely acknowledged that the current practices for ensuring that [mentor teachers] are professionally prepared for their work are inadequate" (Clarke et al., 2014). The collaboration that is the focus of this AR study is strategically designed to unite the university- and school-based teacher educators to provide the PST with a clearer understanding of how theory and practice intersect.

"Third Spaces" in Teacher Education

Both coursework and clinical experiences serve a unique purpose in PSTs path to becoming a teacher. Academic knowledge is the primary focus in coursework, and practical knowledge is modeled and acquired during clinical experiences. These take place in a school setting that has a formal agreement with the university to host PSTs, yet, as with the disconnect between knowledge-types, a relationship between university- and school-based teacher educators is often absent. Third-space theory aims to disrupt the theory/practice divide by suggesting a space in which university- and school-based teacher educators (e.g., mentor teachers) work collaboratively to reconcile theoretical and practical knowledge, and where the benefits of clinical experience can be maximized for PSTs, students, and mentor teachers alike (Beck, 2020; Zeichner, 2010).

This third space provides distinct benefits to each of the stakeholders (Beck, 2020) by promoting the development of thoughtful and reflective practices across the PST, mentor teacher, and university instructor, as well as critical discussion that can lead to "new and shared understanding and practices" (Martin et al., 2011, p. 300). Unquestionably, key stakeholders in both university and school contexts must play a role in the promotion of robust third spaces for PSTs. University-based teacher educators must work alongside school-based teacher educators (e.g., mentor teachers and administrators) to design structured opportunities for PSTs to use knowledge in action and highlight the interplay between course content and field experiences (Darling-Hammond & Bransford, 2007; Goodlad, 1984; Grossman et al., 2009; Martin & Mulvihill, 2020). Mentoring is complex, and school-based teacher educators play a myriad of roles, including "instructional coach, emotional support system, and socializing agent" (Butler & Cuenca, 2012), and the success of PSTs can be attributed largely to the quality of their experiences alongside their mentors (Clarke et al., 2014). Therefore, the aim of this action research is to enhance the quality of the clinical experiences for PSTs.

CONTEXT

This AR study includes partners from Arizona State University's Mary Lou Fulton Teachers' College and Miller Child Development Center (pseudonym, henceforth referred to as Miller). ASU's MLFTC enrolled just over 2,100 undergraduate students in Fall of 2019 and has more than a hundred full-time faculty members and hundreds of partner schools. Miller, a Head Start preschool, is one of MLFTC's partner schools within which preservice teachers in teacher education programs complete their program's clinical internship or student teaching requirements. Head Start programs, including Miller, are designed to provide wraparound services (i.e., health, nutrition, and education) for young children experiencing poverty (NHSA, n.d.). Miller Head Start's philosophy is based on the following tenets: "Positive interactions and relationships with adults provide a critical foundation for successful learning. Social-emotional competence is a significant factor in school success. Constructive, purposeful play supports essential learning. The physical environment affects the type and quality of learning interactions. Teacher-family partnerships promote development and learning" (Teaching Strategies, 2022).

Miller is a free preschool program for children ages 3–5, including children with disabilities. Students' parents or guardians must meet income eligibility requirements for Head Start and live in a designated geographic area. Children and their families receive comprehensive services to meet their educational, social, health, nutritional, and emotional needs. The program operates Monday-Friday, 8:15 AM to 2:30 PM. Miller includes six classrooms, six lead teachers, six assistant teachers, one inclusion specialist, one education coordinator, one director and one administrative assistant. The program enrolls approximately 90 children ages 3–5. Of these, only one of the six lead teachers and the education coordinator hold bachelor's degrees in Early Childhood Education. The director has a bachelor's degree in a field unrelated to education.

METHODS

AR is a robust research approach that has the potential to activate change by merging theory and practice using a rigorous methodology. AR is cyclical in nature, with "a non-linear structure that emphasizes a recursive research process" (Mertler, 2020, p. 17). While there are many AR models, each involves implementing an action that becomes the basis of the next AR cycle (e.g., Mills, 2018; Stringer, 2007). Beginning with a problem of practice, action researchers conduct cycles of research—they observe, collect and synthesize data, develop an intervention, act, and repeat (Mertler, 2020). As the action researcher rotates through each cycle, they build on what has been learned in the previous cycle. In this way, AR is never complete, but is instead a process of never-ending beginnings (Trunk Sirca & Shapiro, 2007). That said, AR is a strong research approach with each cycle grounded in both prior findings as well as relevant theory. Research questions, methods, and analysis are aligned to epistemological, methodological, and conceptual frameworks (Herr & Anderson, 2005; Noffke, 2009) and the local context. Another distinguishing feature is the role of the researcher, a practitioner in the research setting with intimate first-hand knowledge of the context and a stake in the outcome of the research. AR does not strive for generalization, but instead seeks to advance outcomes and understandings within the researcher's immediate context.

This chapter will describe the first two cycles of this AR study. The overarching research is driven by the problem of practice identified when we initially embarked on this study: the disconnect between university coursework and internship experiences (i.e., theoretical knowledge and practical knowledge) for PSTs. In this AR study, university-based teacher educators are university faculty. The school-based teacher educators are the Miller teachers and will be referred to as mentor teachers. Mentor teachers serve a specific purpose in teacher education programs, as they serve as both the classroom teacher, as well as a guide and coach for PSTs. Cycle 1 was a reconnaissance cycle, in which data were collected from relevant stakeholders and the researchers explored prior related research to further articulate the challenge and consider potential solutions to address some facet of the problem. Cycle 2 consisted of the implementation of the co-developed three-pronged innovation and data collection to determine the efficacy of the innovation for PSTs and mentor teachers alike. For each cycle, we describe the intervention, research questions, data collection and synthesis, findings, and discuss the next cycles of the intervention.

ACTION RESEARCH CYCLE 1

The purpose of Cycle 1 was to assess the needs of university and Miller stakeholders to co-create an experience supportive of both PSTs and Miller teachers, inclusive of teachers that served as mentor teachers and those who did not. Therefore, Cycle 1 focused on reconnaissance, including a literature review and information-gathering from the local context, and AR questions include:

RQ1: What would support mentor teachers (particularly those without bachelor's degrees in education) to provide mentoring and robust, meaningful feedback to PSTs?

RQ2: What role(s) might university faculty play in supporting the development of theory-based knowledge for Miller teachers, and to connect theory and practice?

Cycle 1 Participants

Participants in Cycle 1 included the Director and the Education Coordinator of the Miller Child Development Center. The Director was in her 11th year in this role at Miller, after having spent several years in the private sector in a business-oriented occupation. The Director's role is to ensure adherence to Head Start program mandates and to offer leadership that maximizes resources and partnerships to achieve high quality programming for children and their caregivers. The Education Coordinator works under the supervision of the Head Start Director oversees and directs the planning, organizing, and implementation of education services for children. Her role is to support the lead teachers to promote social competence in children and the recognition and enhancement of parents as the primary educators of their children.

Cycle 1 Data Collection

During Cycle 1, there were face-to-face meetings with university and Miller stakeholders, as well as internal meetings among university faculty and administrators. Data were collected through meeting notes, records of members in attendance, points of discussion, and decisions made. Additionally, an activity log of meetings, email contacts and site visits were used to document major activities.

Cycle 1 Results

In fall 2018 the Director of Miller Child Development Center, located in a large urban city in the Southwest U.S., reached out to the ECE program at a large 4-year institution in the same region with the request to pursue a partnership. Representatives from the ECE program visited with the Miller Director. The Director explained that most of their teachers did not hold bachelor's degrees (at the time only one had earned a 4-year degree) and shared that they were seeking assistance in retaining current teachers, attracting new teachers, supporting instructional practices to "reduce unwanted behaviors," and increasing parent participation (meeting notes, October 17, 2018).

Concurrently, ECE faculty within the university were engaging in discussions around the need for high-quality early childhood internship sites where PSTs would have clear guidance and feedback in applying their knowledge of child development and developmentally appropriate practices to a birth to five classroom setting. PSTs were required to complete field service experiences in both a birth to five setting and a Kindergarten to third grade (K–3) setting. As the largest university-based teacher education program in the country, we are faced with challenges due to the scale of our program. There had been persistent challenges in partnering with high-quality birth to age 5 settings, due to the wide variety of early childhood school structures (e.g. Head Start, school-district based, stand-alone centers) and the type of preparation mentor teachers had—or lacked. Another implication of the scale of the program is the reality that many mentees do not see their university supervisor in person. Video-based supervision was the norm as PSTs were completing internships in sites across the region, meaning PSTs meet with their faculty supervisor virtually for a pre-conference to review the lesson plan before implementing it. Then, PSTs record and submit a 10–15-minute video of themselves teaching the lesson. Finally, a post-conference occurs in which the PST and faculty supervisor meet virtually to debrief based on these videos. This pre- and post-conference cycle occurs two times. The reality is that university faculty had few, if any, opportunities to become familiar with the context in which the PSTs were completing their internship, and they likely did not have relationships with the mentor teachers or administrators. The faculty were seeking internship sites who were interested in developing mutually beneficial relationships and with the aim to co-create more robust clinical experiences for PSTs.

As conversations between the stakeholders progressed, it became evident that a collaborative approach was desirable to all. The Miller Director was explicit about what she hoped to gain from the experience; her focus was supporting her teachers in implementing high-quality practices to support prosocial behaviors in the classroom (meeting notes, January 10, 2019). The Miller leadership requested external support for the faculty, especially around the integration of instructional practices to promote prosocial behavior.

As a result of the meetings, university faculty identified a discrepancy between the language used in the university classroom and the way in which mentor teachers described their decision making and instructional practices. University stakeholders proposed having university faculty routinely on-site to help reconcile these, and other discrepancies and "model how to connect PSTs knowledge from the university classroom to their instructional practices" (meeting notes, November 16, 2018). Additionally, these visits would support engagement between faculty and mentor teachers at the site.

In preparation for the internships with embedded faculty presence to start, the Miller Director and the ECE Coordinator offered university faculty a tour of classrooms with the intention of deepening their understanding of the context. University faculty met and briefly talked with Miller lead teachers, including those who would eventually serve as mentor teachers. The university faculty felt the reconnaissance phase included the voice of key stakeholders, namely Miller leaders, Miller teachers, university faculty and university administrators. It would later become evident that the voice of the Miller faculty had not been sufficiently included in the initial planning cycle. This oversight would set the stage for later tension.

Cycle 1 Conclusion

Data collected during Cycle 1 revealed the priorities for the university-based teacher education program and leadership at the partner site. The collaborative nature of Cycle 1 enabled the stakeholders to co-develop an approach that aimed to meet their interrelated needs. The Miller leadership prioritized providing instructional support, especially around promoting prosocial behaviors. They indicated this type of engagement would support their goal of reducing teacher turnover and improving outcomes for students. The university stakeholders identified their priority as designing a high-quality field experience where PSTs were supported to connect theoretical and practical knowledge. The three-part plan described in Cycle 2 is the result of these Cycle 1 findings.

ACTION RESEARCH CYCLE 2

Cycle 2 Introduction

Two university faculty (Authors 1&2) who participated in the Cycle 1 information-gathering and planning moved forward to co-design, implement, and study an enhanced internship experience for Cycle 2 of this AR. The purpose of Cycle 2 was to embed university faculty alongside mentor teachers and PSTs and explore outcomes for PSTs and mentor teachers. Based on Cycle 1 findings, they began to (1) design and implement an introductory session to become acquainted and build a shared language among PSTs and their mentor teachers, (2) implement an enhanced clinical experience for PSTs, and (3) foster their relationships with Miller teachers. The aim of this model, implemented in Cycle 2 based on Cycle 1 findings, was to help bridge the theory to practice gap in clinical experiences in an early childhood setting by supporting PSTs and mentor teachers alike.

Cycle 2 Participants

Cycle 2 participants included four mentor teachers at Miller and four PSTs. The PSTs self-selected to complete their internship at Miller. The Miller leadership identified four mentor teachers to host the PST interns from among those who met the university criterion for a mentor teacher (i.e., a minimum of three years teaching experience). These four were receptive to hosting a PST in their classroom.

Cycle 2 Intervention

Cycle 2 action steps involved implementing a three-pronged intervention: an introductory session with mentor teachers and PSTs, the on-site presence of university faculty in classrooms, and university faculty supervision of PSTs.

Introductory meeting with mentor teachers. The first feature of the intervention was an event for the four mentor teachers to become acquainted with university faculty and the four PSTs. University faculty showed a short documentary highlighting trauma in early childhood and the implications for behavior, as well as the long-term impact of trauma on well-being. This was followed by a short presentation on resilience and a facilitated discussion.

Embedding University Faculty. The second unique feature of this intervention is embedding university faculty (Authors 1&2) in the classrooms alongside mentor teachers and PSTs. The PSTs were on site, a minimum of four hours two times a week. University faculty (i.e., Authors 1&2) were on site in classrooms one day a week for two-hours, with the intent to collaborate with mentor teachers, model strategies for PSTs, and provide feedback and ongoing support as PSTs make connections between theory and practice. University faculty planned to step into the lead teacher role (e.g. to lead whole group time, facilitate center time) to allow time for mentor teachers and PSTs to collaborate and have protected time for mentor teachers to provide feedback that would support PSTs development. In addition, they planned to model strategies for PSTs during teacher-child interactions (e.g., expanding language, asking open ended questions). University faculty were also to observe and offer feedback on planned PST lessons and their enactment, suggest materials and strategies, as well as point out strategies the mentor teacher employed which aligned theory to practice.

University Faculty Supervising PSTs. The third unique feature of the intervention, which is the focus of this AR cycle, is the supervisory role of the full time university faculty in the clinical experience. University supervisors are typically either current or former (e.g., retired) Early Childhood Educators, hired on a part-time, per PST basis, rather than being full time university faculty. This is not unique to our particular university context, and presents challenges as university supervisors that do not teach in the teacher education program are often unfamiliar with the associated academic coursework and therefore rely heavily on their own teaching experience (Valencia et al., 2009). Further, university supervisors in our context typically have only two structured interactions with PSTs, and never enter into the internship classrooms. Typically, the PST submits a lesson plan and video recording of themselves teaching prior to each of the structured interactions. With the model that is the focus of this AR research, full-time university faculty are supervising with the aim to offer PSTs real-time feedback on the connections between coursework and classroom experiences.

Author 1 took on the role of university supervisor for all four of the PSTs, and was therefore able to see the PSTs weekly in the classrooms. This afforded her the opportunity to create a role that was distinct from that of other university supervisors. Author 1 was able to see PSTs interact with students and engage with mentor teachers. Further, she provided support to PSTs around lesson planning with the contextual knowledge about the curriculum, the classroom, and students. The aim was also to build robust relationships for providing feedback that pushed PSTs to take risks and create innovative classroom experiences that meaningfully engage children while meeting expectations of course work.

Cycle 2 AR Questions

RQ1: To what extent were university-based TE supporting PSTs to bridge theory and practice in clinical experiences?

RQ2: How and to what extent were relationships between university TE (i.e., faculty) and school-based TE (i.e., mentor teachers) fostered?

Cycle 2 Data Collection

Four data sources were leveraged to address Cycle 2 research questions. First, university faculty developed post-internship reflection prompts for PSTs to complete each week to document their activities during their internship time (e.g., observations, teaching lessons, teacher child-interactions, whole groups). The PSTs documented what type of feedback, if any, they received and from whom (e.g., mentors, university faculty). PSTs also included any questions they had for university faculty.

As a second source of qualitative data, university faculty (Authors 1 & 2) completed weekly structured post-internship journaling. They recorded observations and interactions with PSTs and mentors, including descriptions of their own activities that week (e.g. observations of PSTs, engaging in teacher child-interactions, stepping into teacher roles) as well the activities of PSTs and other adults in the classroom (e.g. assessment, small or whole group teaching). University faculty also documented how the PSTs experiences connect to coursework and feedback they provided to PSTs. Additionally, feedback given to PSTs by their mentor teacher was documented, along with descriptions of if/when university faculty stepped into teaching roles to support release time for the mentor teacher to meet with PSTs.

The third source of data was a summative survey completed by PSTs. PSTs were surveyed about their internship experiences and interactions with mentors, the children, as well as the connection between coursework and applied assignments at their internship site.

Finally, to complement these reflections and surveys Author 1 conducted a focus group interview at the end of the semester with the mentor teachers to gain feedback and perspectives on their experiences as mentors at the conclusion of Cycle 2.

Cycle 2 Results

RQ 1: Enhanced Clinical Experience for PSTs. Mentor teachers seemed to welcome university faculty modeling of strategies for PSTs. For example, "expanding children's language, asking open ended questions, and managing behaviors in the classroom" (Author 2 Post Internship Journal). Mentor teachers, however, did not engage university faculty in leading whole group activities, which would have provided a time for mentors and PSTs to collaborate. There was potentially a miscommunication around the role of the university faculty in the classroom, which led mentors to underutilize them as a resource. For example, the data indicated that mentor teachers were routinely providing PSTs with feedback; however, the university faculty did not observe this happening while in the classrooms. In just over 80% of documented visits by university faculty, mentor teachers were not observed providing feedback to PSTs. It is possible mentor teachers chose to give that role to university faculty when they were present. As the semester unfolded, university faculty intentionally shifted to take a less active role with mentors and a more involved role with PSTs, observing PST teacher-child interactions during planned PST lessons, offering "feedback on lessons, making suggestions for materials and strategies, as well as pointing out strategies the mentor teacher employed aligning theory to practice" (Author1 Post Internship Journal).

The embedded university faculty were uniquely situated to support PSTs in making connections between their coursework and application in an authentic setting. During weekly visits, university faculty used a blend of formal feedback and "on-the-fly" feedback during classroom transitions or momentary breaks (Author2 Post Internship Journal). PSTs were asked to reflect on their internship experiences with university faculty. This provided a vital opportunity to support students in making explicit connections between what they were observing and their coursework. For example, PST Theresa described literacy activities she had observed in class, she was encouraged to make direct connections between her observations and the literacy course she was currently taking. In another example, PST Theresa was supported to connect her knowledge of low-intensity strategies when "managing conflict between pre-k students, specifically not being too quick to intervene" (Author2 Post Internship Journal). The university faculty's knowledge of the scope and sequence of the teacher education program was instrumental in bridging theory to application during this conversation.

RQ 2: Fostering Relationships. The faculty journals and post interview with mentor teachers revealed some of the success and challenges of hosting an intern as well as their perspective of an embedded internship model. During the first two weeks of visits by faculty at the internship site, the university faculty noticed a hesitancy of mentor teachers as documented by the post-internship structured journal entries. For example, teacher Ashley shared with the university faculty that she was "initially hesitant to have an intern when [Miller director] shared the proposed initiative." Further, teacher Candi described her concern that "student behavior is elevated when other adults are present." University faculty made an effort to step-in, in a support role, by wiping tables, sweeping floors, supporting transitions, and engaging with children during small groups or center-based activities. The aim was to be seen as collaborative partners versus outsiders with evaluative intent. University faculty offered resources to mentors, such as books or materials that aligned with unit themes. Most mentors felt like overall the experience of having the PSTs in their classrooms was positive, they reported enjoying having a new perspective and new ideas shared, also enjoyed getting to know their PST's.

In the post interview, teacher Emma commented that she "really connected" with the PST in her classroom. Others, however, viewed having interns as a burden for example teacher Candi felt pressure to step away from their own students to give PSTs feedback or to prompt PSTs who were hesitant to engage with students to support children during classroom activities. Several logistical challenges were reported including the timing of the internship. Mentor teachers believed they could better integrate the interns in the classrooms if they had begun in the fall rather than the spring. Further, as expected, time to collaborate with the PST's was a challenge when faced with the competing—and often more immediate—needs of students in the classroom. Teacher Emma said "I needed more time to talk with my intern, the interns got there when students arrived and left when kids left, we did not have any time to sit and talk or collaborate while they were here. I did email and text with my intern, but I would like to have more time to collaborate and talk with my intern face to face." Some solutions suggested by the mentor teachers included dedicated time to meet with and collaborate with interns and faculty prior to the start of the internship. When asked about the embedded internship model the mentors reported that they felt like four adults in the classrooms felt overwhelming at times.

DISCUSSION

The recursive and intentional nature inherent to AR was appropriate for this study. Because data were strategically collected each week throughout Cycle 2, the practitioner researchers were able to analyze data and adjust as needed. There was no need to wait until the semester concluded to reflect. For example, it quickly became evident that the voice of important stakeholders was left out of the design and implementation of the intervention. Though we set forth with the intention of including all perspectives, the Miller faculty voice was not present or included from the initial planning cycle. The assumption was that these were aligned with that of the Miller administrators. This assumption was reinforced at the initial introductory meeting when the teachers' opinions expressed on the *Professional*

Development Interest Survey appeared to be aligned with that of the administrators. Had mentor teachers been included in conversations at the inception of the partnership, challenges around both expectations and logistics could have been mitigated. Further, this would have afforded university faculty the opportunity to build a trusting relationship prior to the internship experience by addressing those needs from the start.

Distrust and misunderstandings between university- and school-based teacher educators are well documented (Bullough et al, 1997; Bullough et al., 2004). Further, the role of a mentor teacher is not without its challenges, requiring extensive commitments of time and effort outside of their typical duties (Rajuan et al., 2007). In this instance, the ambiguity of the role of the university faculty and mentor teachers in relation to the PSTs during internships in classrooms may have created tension in the relationships between university faculty and mentors. As previously mentioned, while PSTs reported regularly receiving feedback from mentor teachers, the university faculty did not observe this. A likely explanation for this is that the mentor teachers believed this to be the role of the university faculty when they were in the classrooms. It is possible mentor teachers chose to give that role to university faculty when they were present. Partnerships are complex and resources needed for robust partnerships are extensive (Lillejord & Børte, 2016). From a practical perspective for ECE teacher education, the challenges with creating third spaces for PSTs to bridge theory and practice will persist. However, continued improvements can be made through authentic engagements among school-based sites and university faculty using approaches such as AR that allow for continual implementation, data collection, refinement. AR afforded the university faculty to better understand the context of this particular early education setting, and a critical perspective on how to form meaningful partnerships with mentors that fosters a quality relationship and enhances the experiences of PSTs.

REFERENCES

Beck, J. S. (2020). Investigating the third space: A new agenda for teacher education research. *Journal of Teacher Education, 7*(14), 379–391.

Bullough, R. V., Jr., & Draper, R. J. (2004). Making sense of a failed triad: Mentors, university supervisors, and positioning theory. *Journal of Teacher Education, 55*(5), 407–420.

Bullough, R. V., Jr., Kauchak, D., Crow, N. A. Hobbs, S., & Stokes, D. (1997). Professional development schools: Catalyst for teacher and school change. *Teaching and Teacher Education, 13*(2), 153–169.

Butler, B. M., & Cuenca, A. (2012). Conceptualizing the roles of mentor teachers during student teaching. *Action in Teacher Education, 34*(4), 296–308.

Chetty, R., Friedman, J. N., & Rockoff, J. E. (2014). Measuring the impacts of teachers II: Teacher value-added and student outcomes in adulthood. *American Economic Review, 104*(9), 2633–79.

Clarke, A., Triggs, V., & Nielsen, W. (2014). Cooperating teacher participation in teacher education: A review of the literature. *Review of Educational Research, 84*(2), 163–202.

Cope, P., & Stephen, C. (2001). A role for practicing teachers in initial teacher education. *Teaching and Teacher Education, 17*(8), 913–924.

Darling-Hammond, L. (2009, February). *Teacher education and the American future.* Charles W. Hunt Lecture. Presented at the annual meeting of the American Association of Colleges for Teacher Education, Chicago.

Darling-Hammond, L., & Bransford, J. (2007). *Preparing teachers for a changing world: What teachers should learn and be able to do.* John Wiley & Sons.

Goodlad, J. I. (1984). *A place called school.* McGraw-Hill.

Grossman, P., Hammerness, K., & McDonald, M. (2009b). Redefining teaching, re-imagining teacher education. *Teachers and Teaching: Theory and Practice, 15*(2), 273–289.

Head Start. (2013). Head Start policy & regulations: 1302.91: Staff qualifications and requirements. https://eclkc.ohs.acf.hhs.gov/policy/45-cfr-chap-xiii/1302-91-staff-qualifications-competency-requirements

Herr, K., & Anderson, G. L. (2005). *The action research dissertation: A guide for students and faculty.* SAGE Publications.

Institute of Medicine and National Research Council. (2015). *Transforming the workforce for children birth through age 8: A unifying foundation.* The National Academies Press.

Lewis, E. (2012). Locating the third space in initial teacher training. *Research in Teacher Education, 2*(2), 31–36.

Lillejord, S., & Børte, K. (2016). Partnership in teacher education–a research mapping. *European Journal of Teacher Education, 39*(5), 550–563.

Martin, L. E., & Mulvihill, T. (2020). Voices in education: Professional development schools (PDS): in the rear-view mirror or still a promising model?. *The Teacher Educator, 55*(3), 239–247.

Martin, S. D., Snow, J. L., & Torrez, C. A. F. (2011). Navigating the terrain of Third Space: Tensions with/in relationships in school-university partnerships. *Journal of Teacher Education, 62*(3), 299–311.

Mertler, C. A. (2020). Action research: Improving schools and empowering educators (6th ed.). SAGE.

Mills, G. E. (2018). *Action research: A guide for the teacher researcher* (6th ed.). Pearson.

NAEYC (2019). Professional standards and competencies for early childhood educators. https://www.naeyc.org/sites/default/files/globally-shared/downloads/PDFs/resources/position-statements/standards_and_competencies_ps.pdf

Noffke, S. (2009). Revisiting the professional, personal, and political dimensions of action research. In S. E. Noffke & B. Somekh (Eds.), *The SAGE handbook of educational action research* (pp. 6–24). Sage.

National Head Start Association. (n.d.). *National Head Start Start Association.* Retrieved April 8, 2022. From https://nhsa.org/

Rajuan, M., Beijaard, D., & Verloop, N. (2007). The role of the cooperating teacher: Bridging the gap between the expectations of cooperating teachers and student teachers. *Mentoring & Tutoring, 15*(3), 223–242.

Stringer, E. T. (2007). *Action research* (3rd ed.). Sage.

Teaching Strategies. (2022). *The creative curriculum for preschools.* https://teachingstrategies.com/product/the-creative-curriculum-for-preschool/

Trunk Sirca, N., & Shapiro, A. (2007). Action research and constructivism: Two sides of the same coin? Or, one side?. *International Journal of Management in Education, 1*(1–2), 100–107.

UNESCO. (2020). *Global Education Monitoring Report: Inclusion and education: All means all.* https://en.unesco.org/gem-report/report/2020/inclusion

Valencia, S. W., Martin, S. D., Place, N. A., & Grossman, P. (2009). Complex interactions in student teaching: Lost opportunities for learning. *Journal of Teacher Education, 60*(3), 304–322.

Wylie, C., & Vaughn, K. (2019). *Pathways, labour market experiences, and learning at work and beyond at age 26: A report from the competent learners project.* New Zealand Center for Educational Research. https://www.nzcer.org.nz/research/publications/pathway-labour-market-age-26

Zeichner, K. (2010). Rethinking the connections between campus courses and field experiences in college-and university-based teacher education. *Journal of Teacher Education, 61(1–2)* 88–99.

CHAPTER 6

NOT JUST A MARCH TO TENURE AND PROMOTION

Faculty Careers at a Community College

Eric Hofmann

INTRODUCTION

Full-time faculty often struggle to balance responsibilities, a problem particularly relevant to new faculty on tenure-track lines (Larson et al., 2019; Stupnisky et al., 2017) and at community colleges (Sallee, 2008), where the proportion of non-white students is 11 percentage points higher than in four-year institutions (National Center for Education Statistics, 2019b). Engaging students of diverse backgrounds is imperative in these colleges, but many faculty across higher education lacked graduate school training in this area (Behar-Horenstein et al., 2016; Cassuto, 2017; Elliott & Oliver, 2016). Research on community or 'two-year' colleges (CCs) suggests that support for teaching sustains faculty job satisfaction (Lyons & Akroyd, 2014). With nearly half of U.S. college students enrolled in CCs before the COVID-19 pandemic (American Association of Community Colleges, 2016), improving the faculty experience affects the futures of millions of economically- and socially disadvantaged students who attend these schools.

Institutional factors affect job satisfaction at four-year colleges, including tenure clarity (Ponjuan et al., 2015; Stupnisky et al., 2017) and having tenure (Bozeman & Gaughan, 2011). In 2018–19, only 58% of public CCs had a tenure system, compared with 94% of public four-years (National Center for Education Statistics, 2019a). Meanwhile, a shift to fewer full-time, tenure-track lines is occurring across higher education (Chronicle of Higher Education, 2021), a change Migliaccio and Murphy (2014) attribute to state-level funding decreases and perceptions of post-secondary education as an "individual good rather than a social good," an especially relevant observation given the mission of CCs to meet the needs of under-served students (p. 351). To that end, public four-year colleges spend two-and-a-half times more per full-time student than public two-years (Opportunity America Working Group on Community College Workforce Education, 2020).

The purpose of this study is to examine the relationship between sustained educational development (ED) and tenure-track faculty careers at a two-year college. ED is defined as classroom-focused learning that supports faculty's professional growth and the teaching, scholarship, and service requirements for tenure. Pursuing an academic career at the margins of higher education—the two-year college—presents many challenges. The results of this study suggest that coupling tools to help faculty clarify, integrate, and reflect on their role with support from their peers may improve faculty's experiences and enhance their support for student learning. This practice might also contribute to organizational learning that improves educational attainment for students seeking to (re)connect with the promises of formal education.

BACKGROUND AND CONTEXT

Research suggests that CC faculty can feel marginalized by academic hierarchies (Fugate & Amey, 2000; Gonzales & Ayers, 2018), which might explain why many doctoral students do not consider jobs in this sector (Cassuto, 2017; Terosky & Gonzales, 2016). Research experience is often favored over teaching in CC faculty appointments (Hyson et al., 2021), but because these faculty can be assigned five courses per semester (Gonzales & Ayers, 2018; Migliaccio & Murphy, 2014), the perceived diminished role of scholarship in CCs contributes to lower status (Vitullo & Spalter-Roth, 2013). Given the pedagogical needs of many new faculty, it is important to note a movement toward more demanding research and publication expectations in the two-year sector (Bozeman & Gaughan, 2011; Migliaccio & Murphy, 2014; Virick & Strage, 2016), which can lead to concerns expressed by four-year college faculty regarding clarifying expectations, balancing responsibilities, and forming a faculty identity (Larson et al., 2019). Unclear tenure expectations in CCs may stem from their multi-pronged missions to support education for immediate entry into a job, transfer to a four-year college, and community or continuing education (Elliott & Oliver, 2016; Gonzales & Ayers, 2018).

Studies in four-year colleges have shown that department colleagues influence the faculty experience, such as acknowledging one's work and collaborating on research supports satisfaction (Bozeman & Gaughan's, 2011). Relationships with more senior faculty can provide insight on tenure, but women and underrepresented minority faculty appear to be disadvantaged by less frequent contact with these peers (Hyers et al., 2012). Stupnisky et al. (2017) indicated that 'relatedness' to other faculty within the department can predict junior faculty success in teaching and learning. Faculty members whose priority for teaching or research align with their chair reported more clarity about tenure and promotion (Virick & Strage, 2016); moreover, the belief that talking with a chairperson would lead to tenure both supports faculty's sense of agency and contributes to their satisfaction (Campbell & O'Meara, 2014). Miller and Murry's (2015) study of departments considered 'dysfunctional' suggests that ineffective individual leadership capabilities are a significant source of professional tension. Institutional governance structures often assign department leaders responsibility for student learning; however, there is an acknowledged dearth of scholarship in this area (Hoekstra & Newton, 2017), as most research in teaching and learning leadership is in K–12 contexts (see Drago-Severson, 2009).

Most colleges and universities provide ED structures for their learning mission (Austin & Sorcinelli, 2013; Grant & Keim, 2002; Sorcinelli et al., 2006), but a recent study indicated the absence of formal ED centers in CCs (Eddy et al., 2019). Elliott and Oliver (2016) correlated ED participation in a CC with students' perceptions of faculty effectiveness, and Beaumont (2020) suggested several benefits of cross-disciplinary ED for CC faculty. Sorcinelli et al. (2006) surveyed ED providers in a national organization and surfaced faculty's changing roles and balancing responsibilities as top ED priorities, overall, while ED organizers in CCs identified instruction for under-prepared students, assessment of student learning, and supporting part-time instructors as priorities, with departmental leadership as a high challenge for CCs.

Over time, institutional ED leaders have assumed a range of activities that address faculty roles "peripheral to teaching and learning (e.g., tenure support, personal ePortfolios)" (Benito-Capa et al., 2017, p. 11). A national survey of ED staff indicated that interpersonal skills, career planning, and deeper understanding of teaching skills needed urgent attention (Sanford & Kinch, 2016). However, while faculty may believe ED practices are useful, they may also feel they cannot benefit personally (Hassan, 2011) or that work-life balance limits their participation (Brownell & Tanner, 2012). Effective ED must address faculty's learning needs (Hott & Teitjen-Smith, 2018) and should consider Knowles' (1980) framework of adult learning and theories that have emerged within it, including self-directed (Caffarella, 1993), experiential (Kolb & Kolb, 2009), and transformative learning (Mezirow, 1997). A key component of these strategies is reflection, which Rodgers (2002) identifies as an important learning goal for educator training. Bezard and Shaw (2017) investigated the impact of transformative learning activities on high school instructors' multi-cultural self-awareness and noted the lack of depth in their answers, "indicating underdeveloped personal reflection skills" (p. 43). ED leaders who support faculty's growth might consider implementing ePortfolios, self-authored websites that promote reflection and integrative social pedagogy (Eynon & Gambino, 2017). Portfolio practice has been shown to support adult learners (Brown et al., 2004) and CC tenure processes (Danowitz, 2012).

METHODS

This action research study was conducted at an urban two-year college that enrolls approximately 15,000 students annually and is part of a university system in the Northeast. Its three-year graduation rate hovers around 30%. Students represent nearly 80 heritage languages; 54% are immigrants; and two-thirds receive financial aid. Faculty respondents in two recent cycles of the national Collaborative on Academic Careers in Higher Education (COACHE) job satisfaction survey showed the most dissatisfaction compared with the overall university rating and all CCs. The college employees include nearly 360 tenure-line faculty, 62% who hold doctorates and 66% who have tenure. The university's primary reappointment, promotion, and tenure (RPT) criteria are teaching effectiveness, scholarly work, and service to the department and college. Student advisement and collegiality are also focus areas, while leadership is an additional component of promotion to associate and full professor, the latter which affords financial rewards and exemption from annual evaluation processes.

Participants

Cycle 1 interview participants included eight full-time faculty promoted to full professor between 2010 and 2019 representing seven academic departments. Current or former department chairpersons were excluded. Except for one participant, all chose a name that represents their gender expression: two men and five women. Three of the interview participants were born outside the U. S., and two are first-generation Americans, as determined from interviews, workplace conversations, or public documents. This identity is particularly relevant given the large immigrant student population at the college. Results from online surveys completed by 47 tenure-track faculty at the rank of assistant, associate, or lecturer (faculty may be promoted to associate professor before achieving tenure) supported interview findings but are not discussed here. All participants were recruited through an email list of faculty compiled from the college's online directory.

Cycle 2 participants included eight faculty and senior staff who have facilitated ED seminars in the past five years. The first six faculty and two teaching center staff who responded were selected for this design team (DT) under the condition that no more than two faculty would participate from a single department. Five academic departments were represented. Six women and two men participated; five were born outside the U. S. Recruitment email lists were compiled from an internal database of ED leaders in the last five years. Additionally, current and former elected chairpersons in the past five years attended a demonstration of the digital planning tool. Seven of the 15 who met the criteria responded to the call. The six who attended represented four departments; half were women and at least four were born outside the U. S.

Data Collection

Cycle 1 included semi-structured, one-hour interviews conducted via video conferencing. The protocol included questions about participants' graduate training, supportive college relationships, ED participation, and notable obstacles and supports for their work. Participants also provided select annual evaluation materials, typically 10-page formal reports that addressed their individual progress toward the university's tenure requirements.

Formal data collection in Cycle 2 included three online surveys: an initial two-question survey of DT members, a final survey with six Likert-type and four short-answer questions adapted from Kans' (2021) evaluation of an academic engineering department's program development process, and a survey of the demo participants that included the same six Likert-type and four different short-answer questions. All but one demo participant answered the survey. Additional instruments included a SWOT analysis co-constructed by the DT, assessment of the digital portfolio tool using a rubric the researcher constructed, and field notes from all 10 online meetings.

Data Analysis

Interviews were transcribed by an automated online service, Temi.com, and cleaned by the researcher. Open-coding with the NVivo12 software package generated three overarching themes and eight first-level subthemes representing the coding tree approach for semi-structured interviews identified by Harrell and Bradley (2009). For the purposes of this article, Cycle 1 findings are limited to the broad themes. Themes and subthemes were compared against participants' evaluation materials, which were also coded to identify references of ED activities across all RPT categories. Short-answer items in Cycle 2 surveys were open-coded manually, with descriptive statistics applied to quantitative items.

Trustworthiness and Quality Assurance

Trustworthiness was established along several dimensions described by Lincoln and Guba (1985). Credibility was established primarily through methods and source triangulation, such as comparing interview participants' statements with promotion documents and connecting themes across sources. Member checking helped confirm the accuracy of transcribed interviews and reinforced Cycle 1 findings (Brit et al., 2016), as did seeking negative evidence during coding processes (Miles et al., 2019, p. 259). Frequent interactions with a faculty advisor helped address the criterion of research dependability, as did sharing meeting notes with participants and holding separate DT meetings with some because of scheduling challenges, which helped verify and probe themes that surfaced. Finally, confirmability was met by incorporating reflexive practices throughout the data collection and analysis processes. Because the values-laden nature of Action Research complicates neutrality (Morse, 2015), frequent analytic memo-ing supported critical reflection and helped document the data analysis process.

Findings

Three findings about CC academic roles emerged in Cycle 1: the challenges of CC academic careers, resources that support faculty success, and strategies that help faculty conceptualize their role. Overall, these data demonstrated that RPT success at this college hinges on embracing one's identity as a CC faculty member. For example, Zara acknowledged arriving at the college with "all [her] community college clichés" after completing a post-doctorate assignment. Jon Michael cautioned tenure-track candidates about "having this mindset of what academia should be based on what their doctoral programs are," saying one needs to "think about your career in the long term, not just a march to tenure and promotion." Participants noted a lack of balance, lack of clarity, and lack of preparation for themselves or colleagues in various aspects of the job.

Faculty found support from colleagues and departmental chairpersons, and through ED opportunities. Clyde said, "If you don't have somebody . . . you're talking to regularly about this . . . it's very easy to miss." Tomar discussed how she connected several college initiatives learned about through ED activities: "It was a result of a discussion with other colleagues." Asked if ED participation had an impact on any aspect of her job, Linda shared this: "Oh, everything… My teaching has changed dramatically." Emma became interested in how ED might help her peers and her learn their role: "What makes you an academic? . . . And I think over time I've become better. I've understood a little bit of what it means to have a specific pedagogy." Several mentioned that chairs recommended ED participation, but faculty were split about the appropriateness of saying no to recommendations from more senior colleagues. All indicated having more than one chairperson during their time on the tenure pathway.

Learning as an ongoing part of participants' careers emerged as key to faculty success. Otter encouraged faculty to share their scholarship with students "because they're excited about learning themselves" and emphasized the importance for the college to "nurture that." Emma observed that, "If you're not self-directed and highly-motivated, you are going to struggle when you start at [this college]." Zara proposed this strategy: "Faculty at year one…you should be constantly experimenting with trajectory, ideas, studying the college's strategic plan, mission, and goals. Then, perhaps in year three onwards, you can start aligning your interests towards these larger ideas." Jon Michael noted that faculty work is "always about constant revision and reflection and thinking through what you are actually doing." Asked about the effectiveness of reflection activities on ED, however, Otter said they did not hit the mark: "It was, 'OK, now we'll reflect on this . . . we have about five minutes' . . . No, I don't think it's real reflection."

Figure 6.1 illustrates a conceptual framework for considering how faculty participation in sustained professional learning is a success strategy in a CC. The first column represents faculty's description of their ED experiences; the arrows indicate alignment with their primary responsibilities at the college. ED participation also supported a balanced approach to the myriad responsibilities of teaching, scholarship, and service. Applying this framework to build a resource to help new tenure-track faculty in a CC was the goal of Cycle 2.

Cycle 2 activities were designed to construct a tool to help junior faculty identify and integrate their responsibilities. This was achieved by a design team (DT) of experienced staff and faculty ED leaders who developed a digital template—an ePortfolio—for faculty to document and reflect on their experiences, identify strategies and resources to help them achieve more balance, and assess their professional learning experiences in relation to their personal goals. Two DT members presented a prototype to current and former department chairpersons—those who comprise the college-wide RPT committee—and then collectively investigated the perceived viability for using the tool with junior faculty.

Data analysis surfaced greater understanding of the faculty role and the conditions that help or hinder faculty success described below in more detail. First, a well-designed tool serves multiple purposes but has limitations. Maximizing any tool's value depends on the user's needs and inclinations. Second, colleagues will influence the tool's impact. Chairpersons and peers within and outside the depart-

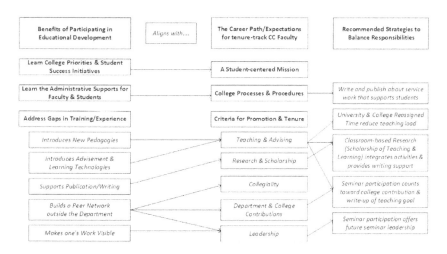

FIGURE 6.1. Faculty Learning as a Strategy for Community College Career Success

ment offer advice that may or may not prove beneficial. Finally, a learner-centered approach challenges the more common method of 'templating.' Every faculty member brings a unique set of passions, strengths, and needs to the college—institutions must embrace faculty's individuality while helping them connect their activities intentionally with larger institutional goals.

Targeted Use

Crafting a template to meet many objectives was a challenge. A survey question about potential benefits of the tool surfaced DT participants' insights on how it might benefit new faculty, with "documenting," "guiding," and "reflecting" noted by at least half the team. Subsequent survey responses to the same six Likert-type questions surfaced distinctions between the DT and chairs' perceptions of the tool at this prototype stage (Table 1). Both groups ranked the tool high for planning and documenting while giving equal weight to its other functions: reflection and integration. An additional benefit expressed by a participant in the demonstration ('demo') highlighted the tool's potential to help faculty "focus energy and time, and to avoid doing too many activities and becoming overwhelmed." Item #3 ranked in the bottom for each group, suggesting that the benefits of tool usage might dissipate over time—it seems best for new faculty. Rankings between the groups differed most with regard to the value of ED and identifying departmental colleagues who would benefit from its use.

Demo participants indicated ideal ePortfolio users: faculty who need help organizing and connecting their work, who are self-directed, or who might need support reflecting on their interests or passions. One of the three who addressed self-direction indicated that "most faculty would not do the extra work," thus revealing a perspective that favors product over process—a focus on immediate goals versus the arc of a career and one's emergent professional identity. Self-direction, however, was viewed by one DT participant as a success strategy by noting the need to help faculty "addresses the nature of how to deal with very little direction." Regarding helping faculty who might need support reflecting on their interests or passions, one chair wrote the following: "Would everyone use it or use it to its fullest potential? Probably not, but simply having a holistic approach suggested and outlined for them could only be beneficial."

Peer Influence

Data analysis reinforced the significant impact of experiences at the departmental level. Responses in the final DT survey revealed participants' understanding of departmental variations in RPT practices, the need for guidance or mentoring, and issues of equity and transparency. Awareness of the chairperson's impact surfaced prominently in meeting discussions, survey responses, and the SWOT analysis, as shown here: "Chairs may perceive [the tool] as a threat to their power and not support its use." Another perceived threat was that using the ePortfolio

TABLE 6.1. Perceptions of the Digital Tool: Design Team Members and Chairpersons

		Design Team (N=8)	Chairs (N=5)	
		M (Rank)	M (Rank)	+/-
1.	The ePortfolio template provides a platform for new faculty to plan and document their activities effectively.	4.63 (2)	4.40 (1)	0.23
2.	The ePortfolio template provides structure for new faculty to reflect regularly on their own professional growth.	4.63 (2)	4.00 (2)	0.63
3.	Regardless of their professorial rank, all full-time faculty can benefit from using this ePortfolio template.	3.63 (6)	3.60 (5)	0.03
4.	The ePortfolio template will help new and junior faculty integrate their professional responsibilities.	4.63 (2)	4.00 (2)	0.63
5.	The ePortfolio will help new and junior faculty consider beneficial ways to incorporate educational development activities in their work.	4.25 (5)	4.00 (2)	0.25
6.	I know colleagues in my department who would benefit from using the tool.	4.75 (1)	3.60 (5)	1.15

SCALE: 5=Strongly Agree, 4=Agree, 3=Neutral, 2=Disagree, 1=Strongly Disagree
Note: One demo attendee did not participate in the survey.

"may feel redundant if chairs don't use it." The demo participants indicated they would consider sharing the template with junior faculty; however, only one referred to the role the chair might play: "Without regular guidance, or if the faculty member disregards the chairperson's guidance, the purpose of the template will be lost."

The SWOT emphasized the highly political nature of promotion and tenure. It is understandable that a chairperson would assess the potential for any instrument they might endorse; what was less clear was how some chair's view peer learning, as evidenced by a debate at the demo about including authentic re-appointment samples in the template. One chairperson suggested this might violate personnel policies, which elicited a response in the Zoom chat from a former chair: "I'm curious—if I choose to share something in my evaluation, don't I have that right?" Told that many faculty share their documents (a practice noted in both cycles of data collection), participants continued to debate. This exchange reinforced Cycle 1 findings about the lack of clarity and transparency around HR policies connected to the RTP process—even some chairs are unclear. Additionally, on the Likert-type questions, chairs ranked lowest their ability to identify departmental faculty who might benefit from using the tool; in contrast, DT members scored it highest, with the 1.15 difference in means suggesting the importance of peer relationships. As one DT participant acknowledged, "If and when I have the opportunity to mentor junior faculty, I am very likely to use this tool if it's available." Another was more strategic about the vital role of department leaders in supporting this work, indicating at the final meeting to "go back to the Chairs so they know they are still part of this development."

A Learner-Centered Approach

Assessment with a self-constructed rubric measured the template's potential in three areas: content related to RPT categories, application of adult learning theories, and alignment with Cycle 1 findings. The aspect of learning that surfaced most often related to reflection, with variations on the word appearing 42 times across the prototype; transformative learning was hardly evident. During the final DT meeting, a participant noted, "Everyone is a case study," thereby emphasizing an important understanding of the faculty role: Even with policies and mentorship, learning must be personalized. Reflecting on one's professional experiences may catalyze a range of responses sending faculty down different paths; those facilitating these processes must adapt to each user. The participant who described a "case study" approach added that because the tool would not be mandatory, it should be included in ED seminars and the new faculty seminar. Another suggested that "the personal portfolio offers faculty a consistent, private, well-designed space to reflect, rather than allowing their reflections to float around in other documents or portfolios that they write in once but never look at again."

Implementing the tool in conjunction with ED activities would link faculty learning spaces explicitly to the RPT path. In this respect, a tool that includes a few guiding prompts in each area would promote a type of 'open pedagogy,' emphasizing the individualized nature of the faculty learning process and the need for routine spaces for guided reflection. A final reflection about one participant's learning from the action steps linked the RPT process with the purpose of ED directly: "It's been a good reminder of how the [evaluation] process can detract from what should be the real goals of the tenure-track process, i.e. growth, reflection on, and demonstration of varied contributions and achievements."

Discussion

This study confirmed the complexity of the CC faculty role by addressing the possibilities and limitations of a resource to guide faculty's growth as successful practitioners while identifying factors that support the tool's effective use. First, Cycle 1 responses reinforced the literature suggesting CC roles are not highly sought (Cassuto, 2017; Terosky & Gonzales, 2016), supporting the need for reflection on one's academic identity. This study also supports findings in the CC literature about difficult transitions to tenure-track jobs because of the lack of preparation (Elliott & Oliver, 2016; Hyson et al., 2021), role clarity (Gonzales & Ayers, 2018) and work-life balance (Sallee, 2008). Findings contribute evidence about the shift to higher research demands on the CC tenure-track (Bozeman & Gaughan, 2011; Migliaccio & Murphy, 2014), thus countering perceptions of CCs as predominantly teaching-focused institutions (Vitullo & Spalter-Roth, 2013) and aligning with recommendations from Hyson et al. (2021) about the importance of ED and educational research in these settings. Acknowledging that clear tenure guidelines support smoother transitions for new faculty (Stupnisky et al., 2017), the ePortfolio's structure includes an introduction to each RPT area and encourages planning, reflecting on, and integrating faculty's activities into a cohesive annual narrative, a practice suggested at other CCs to help document, reflect, and showcase faculty accomplishments (Danowitz, 2012).

This study also demonstrated the highly social and political nature of tenure (Chronicle of Higher Education, 2021) and contributes to literature about the role of colleagues in academic careers (Bozeman & Gaughan, 2011; Hyers et al., 2012; Stupnisky et al., 2017). It builds research specific to CCs (Beaumont, 2020) but goes further by suggesting supportive peers can be found outside one's home department. More so, findings support the importance of the chairperson's role in the RPT process (Campbell & O'Meara, 2014; Virick & Strage, 2016), with data from the demo activity reinforcing the perceived locus of power in departments (Bradley & Bradley, 2010; Miller & Murry, 2015). The extant research appears silent about the impact on junior faculty when a new chairperson is elected, a reality shared by every Cycle 1 interview participant. In this respect, the tool provides a comprehensive picture of the faculty member's journey and may highlight important aspects of faculty work for mentors and chairs.

Finally, this study discerned important relationships between formal ED activities and full-time CC faculty careers, including the role of ED to assist faculty in addressing the complex nature of their role, to support mentorship, and to enhance faculty's identity as expert learners.

Findings support research about the expansion of ED activities over the past quarter-century to address a range of faculty professional needs (Austin & Sorcinelli, 2013). DT participants suggested using the tool in ED seminars for facilitators to learn about participants' goals and help them make connections, thus promoting an 'open pedagogy' that emphasizes the individualized nature of faculty learning (Hott & Tietjen-Smith, 2018). Linking learning spaces directly with the faculty path makes ED more meaningful (Hassan, 2011) and reinforces the value of ePortfolio as a process of integrative, social learning (Enyon & Gambino, 2017). This study also illustrates the value of reflection for educators (Bezard & Shaw, 2017; Rogers, 2002). While the findings address self-directed (Caffarella, 1993) and experiential (Kolb & Kolb, 2009) aspects of adult learning for educators, the ePortfolio prompts do not explicitly address transformative learning (Mezirow, 1997). There is some evidence, however, that the prototype supports faculty examining their professional self-concept and reflecting on the various aspects of their work. To that end, the action steps pave the way for teaching center staff and faculty who facilitate formal seminars to help faculty question their assumptions about the college and its students and make connections across RPT areas more intentionally.

In her book summarizing studies on effective K–12 leadership, Drago-Severson (2009) described how the empirically proven strategies of teaming, providing instructors with leadership roles, supporting collegial inquiry, and instructor mentoring create "holding environments" that challenge educators to broaden their perspective and to take risks, thus improving student experiences. Providing ED opportunities for CC faculty and supporting their development as educators are important strategies for a Learning College (O'Banion, 1997), thus bridging the literature of teacher preparation and growth with post-secondary practices. A successful application of the ePortfolio would be for faculty to take ownership of the tool, with others in the college—mentors, chairpersons, ED leaders—creating opportunities for faculty to integrate their ongoing learning into their ever-evolving professional self-concepts. Improving the experiences of these faculty directly affects the futures of millions of students each year.

Although there appears to be a dearth of literature about helping CC faculty integrate their teaching with other areas of their work, this study's findings suggest that a well-designed planning and reflection tool for new faculty—one they can consider with their chairperson or more senior colleague—can help them find meaningful ways to integrate their work while enhancing their efforts to support student learning. At the same time, the tool provides ED leaders with insights about their participants, thus contributing to collective learning across the institution. The role of CC faculty is important for many reasons, most of all as determinants of success for college students who are treated as second-class citizens if funding models are seen as a measure of perceived value. New avenues for research might include administrators like myself with responsibility for supporting these faculty, and graduate school educators responsible for preparing future faculty.

Limitations

Study limitations are related primarily to participation, as the data include the perspectives of only those who chose to participate. This was especially notable in the Cycle 2 demo with current and former chairpersons, where only seven of the 15 eligible participants responded and only five of the six who attended completed the survey. Additionally, there was no representation throughout from one academic department that houses high-enrollment job-focused majors; similarly, most faculty participants held doctorates, which indicates more traditional faculty training than the overall faculty employee demographics. The impact of the researcher's positionality as a college administrator limited interview participation to faculty whose rank protected them from reprisal, thus in-depth inquiry with junior faculty was lacking. A priority to preserve participant confidentiality limited some details that might support deeper understanding of these issues, particularly with small sample sizes. Finally, the study reveals perceptions of a faculty resource without capturing the experience of implementation; additional research with junior faculty using the tool might bolster these findings.

Implications for Practice

Levin and Greenwood (2011) posit the Action Research methodology as a "strategy" for a new model of knowledge production that responds to the politics of higher education reform precisely because of its participatory and nimble approach to multi-dimensional, 'real-world' issues. Grounding the findings in the literature and the policies, politics, and practices at one CC in a large university system, this study helps to advance the conversation of supporting faculty paths with ED, and highlights the value of the Action Research methodology on stakeholder's learning. This understanding was captured in a DT members' final reflection: "I learned that getting a project in front of the right audience is crucial, and that a key part of succeeding in a multi-stage, longer-term effort is asking for help."

Around the time of the template demo, the university offered funds for campuses to support mid-career faculty seeking promotion to full professor. The provost invited the researcher to meet with several chairpersons to apply for these funds, suggesting the template could be shared with participants. This outcome helps advance the conversation of supporting faculty careers with ED. Additional steps for this project include streamlining the ePortfolio, introducing it to junior faculty to use for reappointment, and connecting it with the next round of the new faculty seminar to evaluate its use. The tool will be shared with staff and faculty facilitators of teaching center seminars to consider explicit connections between these ED spaces and faculty's goals.

The study findings suggest several implications for administrators who have responsibility to support teaching and learning initiatives in large, urban CCs. First, ED practitioners must consider the individual needs and goals of tenure-track faculty; they must understand the pressures of RPT and offer models for how faculty's primary responsibilities might be integrated. Additionally, ED practitioners might work more closely with department chairpersons and senior faculty to design ED activities and promote their value for long-term faculty success and satisfaction. Finally, practitioners in graduate schools might promote CCs as stimulating workplaces with social justice missions. As traditional tenure-track positions disappear, practitioners across the educational spectrum must work together to provide realistic understanding and judgment-free dialogue about equity in educational opportunity and the barriers to achieving it.

REFERENCES

American Association of Community Colleges. (2016). *A national look at community colleges and the students they serve.* https://www.napicaacc.com/docs/AACC_Fact_Sheet_2016.pdf

Austin, A. E., & Sorcinelli, M. D. (2013). The future of faculty development: Where are we going? *New Directions for Teaching and Learning, 2013*(133), 85–97.

Beaumont, J. (2020). Cross-disciplinary professional development at community colleges. *Community College Journal of Research and Practice, 44*(2), 99–116. https://doi.org/10.1080/10668926.2018.1558134

Behar-Horenstein, L. S., Garvan, C. W., Catalanotto, F. A., Su, Y., & Feng, X. (2016). Assessing faculty development needs among Florida's allied dental faculty. *Journal of Dental Hygiene, 90*(1), 52–59.

Benito-Capa, Á., Green, N., Popely, D., Schneiderheinze, A., & Thai-Garcia, P. (2017). Developing faculty to provide university students with improved learning experiences: The role of centers for teaching and learning. *Higher Learning Research Communications, 7*(2), 1–12. https://doi.org/10.18870/hlrc.v7i2.385

Bezard, C., & Shaw, S. A. (2017). Developing multicultural self-awareness through a transformative learning experience. *Journal of Research in Technical Careers, 1*(2), 36–46. http://dx.doi.org/10.9741/2578-2118.1011

Bozeman, B., & Gaughan, M. (2011). Job satisfaction among university faculty: Individual, work, and institutional determinants. *Journal of Higher Education, 82*(2), 154–186.

Bradley, K., & Bradley, J. (2010). Exploring the reliability, validity, and utility of a higher education faculty review process. *Contemporary Issues in Education Research, 3*(4), 21–26. https://doi.org/10.19030/cier.v3i4.193

Brit, L., Scott, S., Cavers, D., Campbell, C., & Walter, F. (2016). Member checking: A tool to enhance trustworthiness or merely a nod to validation? *Qualitative Health Research, 26*(13), 1802–1811.

Brown, J. O., McCrink, C., & Maybee, R. (2004). Beyond college credits: How experiential learning portfolios foster adult students' personal and professional competencies and development. *The Journal of Continuing Higher Education, 52*(3), 24–25. https://doi.org/10.1080/07377366.2004.10400292

Brownell, S. E., & Tanner, K. D. (2012). Barriers to faculty pedagogical change: Lack of training, time, incentives, and tensions with professional identity? *CBE Life Sciences Education, 11*(4), 339–346. https://doi.org/10.1187/cbe.12-09-0163

Caffarella, R. S. (1993). Self-directed learning. *New Directions for Adult and Continuing Education, 57*, 25–36. Jossey-Bass.

Campbell, C. M., & O'Meara, K. (2014). Faculty agency: Departmental contexts that matter in faculty careers. *Research in Higher Education, 55*(1), 49–74.

Cassuto, L. (2017, June 9). A tenure track for teachers? *Chronicle of Higher Education, 63*(38), A39–A40.

Chronicle of Higher Education. (2021). *Rethinking tenure: Abolish, strengthen, or replace it?* The Chronicle of Higher Education Inc.

Danowitz, E. S. (2012). On the right track: Using ePortfolios as tenure files. *International Journal of ePortfolio, 2*(1), 113–124.

Drago-Severson, E. (2009). *Leading adult learning: Supporting adult development in our schools.* Corwin Press.

Eddy, P. L., Hao, Y., Markiewicz, C., & Iverson, E. (2019). Faculty change agents as adult learners: The power of situated learning. *Community College Journal of Research and Practice, 43*(8), 539–555. https://doi.org/10/1080/10668926.2018.1507848

Elliott, R. W., & Oliver, D. E. (2016). Linking faculty development to community college student achievement: A mixed methods approach. *Community College Journal of Research and Practice, 40*(2), 85–99.

Eynon, B., & Gambino, L. (2017). *High impact ePortfolio practice: A catalyst for student, faculty, and institutional learning.* Stylus Publishing, LLC.

Fugate, A. L., & Amey, M. J. (2000). Career stages of community college faculty: A qualitative analysis of their career paths, roles, and development. *Community College Review, 28*(1), 1–22. https://doi.org/10.1177/009155210002800101

Gonzales, L. D., & Ayers, D. F. (2018). The convergence of institutional logics on the community college sector and the normalization of emotional labor: A new theoretical approach for considering the community college faculty labor expectations. *The Review of Higher Education, 41*(3), 455–478.

Grant, M. R., & Keim, M. C. (2002). Faculty development in publicly supported two-year colleges. *Community College Journal of Research and Practice, 26*(10), 793–807.

Harrell, M., & Bradley, M. (2009). *Data collection methods: Semi-structured interviews and focus groups.* RAND Corporation. https://www.rand.org/pubs/technical_reports/TR718.html

Hassan, S. (2011). The needs and perceptions of academics regarding their professional development in an era of educational transformation. *South African Journal of Higher Education, 25*(3), 476–490.

Hoekstra, A., & Newton, P. (2017). Departmental leadership for learning in vocational and professional education. *Empirical Research in Vocational Education and Training, 9*(1), 1–24. https://doi.org/0.1186/s40461-017-0057-0

Hott, B., & Tietjen-Smith, T. (2018). The professional development needs of tenure track faculty at a regional university. *Research in Higher Education Journal, 35,* 1–12.

Hyers, L. L., Syphan, J., Cochran, K., & Brown, T. (2012). Disparities in the professional development interactions of university faculty as a function of gender and ethnic underrepresentation. *Journal of Faculty Development, 26*(1), 18–28.

Hyson, A. R., Bonham, B., Hood, S., Deutschman, M. C., Seithers, L. C., Hull, K., & Jensen, M. (2021). Professional development, shifting perspectives, and instructional change among community college anatomy and physiology instructors. *CBE—Life Sciences Education, 20*(3), 1–13. https://doi.org/10.1187/cbe.21-02-0037

Kans, M. (2021). Engineering education development—A business modelling approach. *Higher Education Evaluation and Development, 15*(1), 53–77. https://doi.org/10.1108/HEED-02- 2020-0003

Knowles, M. S. (1980). *The modern practice of adult education: From pedagogy to andragogy* (2nd ed.). Cambridge Books.

Kolb, A. Y., & Kolb, D. A. (2009). The learning way: Meta-cognitive aspects of experiential learning. *Simulation & Gaming, 40*(3), 297–327.

Larson, L. R., Duffy, L. N., Fenrandez, M., Sturts, J., Gray, J., & Powell, G. M. (2019). Getting started on the tenure track: Challenges and strategies for success. *SCHOLE: A Journal of Leisure Studies and Recreation Education, 34*(1), 36–51. https://doi.org/10.1080/1937156X.2019.1589804

Levin, M., & Greenwood, D. J. (2011). The future of universities: Action research and the transformation of higher education. In P. Reason & H. Bradbury (Eds.), *The SAGE handbook of action research* (pp. 211–226). SAGE Publications, Ltd. https://dx.doi.org/10.4135/9781848607934

Lincoln, Y. S., & Guba, E. G. (1985). *Naturalistic inquiry*. SAGE Publications, Inc.

Lyons, F. W., & Akroyd, D. (2014). The impact of human capital and selected job rewards on community college faculty job satisfaction. *Community College Journal of Research and Practice, 38*(2–3), 194–207. https://doi.org/10.1080/10668926.2014.851965

Mezirow, J (1997). Transformative learning: Theory to practice. *New Directions for Adult and Continuing Education. 1997*(74): 5–12. https://doi.org/10.1002/ace.7401

Migliaccio, T., & Murphy, J. (2014). Do regional associations meet the career needs of teacher-scholars? *The American Sociologist, 45*(2–3), 274–291. http://doi.org/10.1007/s12108-014-9227-8

Miles, M. B., Huberman, A. M., & Saldaña, J. (2019). *Qualitative data analysis: A methods sourcebook* (4th ed.). SAGE Publication Inc.

Miller, M. T., & Murry, J. W., Jr. (2015). Faculty response to department leadership: Strategies for creating more supportive academic work environments. *College Quarterly, 18*(4), 1–8.

Morse, J. M. (2015). Critical analysis of strategies for determining rigor in qualitative inquiry. *Qualitative Health Research, 25*(9), 1212–1222. doi:10.1177/1049732315588501

National Center for Education Statistics. (2019a). *Percentage of degree-granting postsecondary institutions with a tenure system and percentage of full-time faculty with tenure at these institutions, by control and level of institution and selected characteristics of faculty: Selected years, 1993–94 through 2018–19*. https://nces.ed.gov/programs/digest/d19/tables/dt19_316.80.asp

National Center for Education Statistics. (2019b). *Total fall enrollment in degree-granting postsecondary institutions, by level and control of institution and race/ethnicity or nonresident alien status of student: Selected years, 1976 through 2018*. https://nces.ed.gov/programs/digest/d19/tables/dt19_306.20.asp

O'Banion, T. (1997). *A learning college for the 21st century*. Oryx Press.

Opportunity America. (2020, June). *The indispensable institution: Reimagining Community College*. https://opportunityamericaonline.org/indispensable/

Pawson, R., & Tilley, N. (1997). An introduction to scientific realist evaluation. In E. Chelimsky & W. R. Shadish (Eds.), *Evaluation for the 21st century: A handbook* (pp. 405–418). Sage Publications, Inc. https://doi.org/10.4135/9781483348896.n29

Ponjuan, L., Conley, V. M., & Trower, C. (2011). Career stage differences in pre-tenure track faculty perceptions of professional and personal relationships with colleagues. *The Journal of Higher Education, 82*(3), 319–346.

Ponjuan, L., Palomin, L., & Calise. (2015). Latino male ethnic subgroups patterns in college enrollment and degree completion. *New Directions in Higher Education, 172*, 59–67. DOI: 10-1002/HE.

Rodgers, C. R. (2002). Seeing student learning: Teacher change and the role of reflection. *Harvard Educational Review, 72*(2), 230–253.

Sallee, M. W. (2008). Work and family balance: How community college faculty cope. *New Directions for Community Colleges, 2008*(142), 81–91. https://doi.org/10.1002/cc.327

Sanford, R., & Kinch, A. (2016). A new take on program planning: A faculty competencies framework. *The Journal of Faculty Development, 30*(2), 79–96.

Sorcinelli, M. D., Austin, A. E., Eddy, P. L., & Beach, A. L. (2006). *Creating the future of faculty development: Learning from the past, understanding the present.* Jossey-Bass.

Stupnisky, R. H., Hall, N. C., Daniels, L. M., & Mensah, E. (2017). Testing a model of pretenure faculty members' teaching and research success: Motivation as a mediator of balance, expectations, and collegiality. *Journal of Higher Education, 88*(3), 376–400. https://doi.org/10.1080/00221546.2016.1272317

Terosky, A. L., & Gonzales, L. D. (2016). Re-envisioned contributions: Experiences of faculty employed at institutional types that differ from their original aspirations. *Review of Higher Education, 39*(2), 241–268.

Virick, M., & Strage, A. (2016). Perceptions of value-congruence with one's department chair: Does match matter? *The Journal of Faculty Development, 30*(1), 47–56.

Vitullo, M. W., & Spalter-Roth, R. (2013). Contests for professional status: Community college faculty in sociology. *The American Sociologist, 44*(4), 349–65.

CHAPTER 7

STRATEGIC INQUIRY FOR IMPROVING LEARNING AND TEACHING IN AN INTERPROFESSIONAL EDUCATION PROGRAM

Kathryn P. Bell

INTRODUCTION

Interprofessional Education (IPE) is when "when two or more professions learn about, from, and with each other to enable effective collaboration and improve health outcomes" (World Health Organization, 2010). IPE is the educational basis for the movement of healthcare towards a paradigm that embraces interprofessional collaborative practice (IPCP). This idea was introduced in 1972 and has since seen remarkable growth (Brandt, 2015), particularly since the introduction of the Triple Aim (a framework for medicine focused on improving patient outcomes, improving the patient experience, and decreasing cost of care) (Beasley, 2009). More recently, the Quadruple Aim was introduced which adds provider well-being to this paradigm (Bodenheimer & Sinsky, 2014). Today, IPE is widely

Faculty Development: Achieving Change Through Action Research, pages 95–110.
Copyright © 2024 by Information Age Publishing
www.infoagepub.com
All rights of reproduction in any form reserved.

accepted as important for meeting these goals of improved patient outcomes, and indeed is required for inclusion in health professions education programming by many accrediting bodies (Health Professions Accreditors Collaborative, 2019).

While IPE is widely embraced nationally and internationally, questions remain as to the most effective type of IPE training activity or program. This is largely due to the heterogeneity of reported IPE programming (Lapkin et al., 2013). Heterogeneity of programming has been cited as a challenge for drawing conclusions about the effectiveness of programming, however, the importance of individual institutional context has also been identified as a key element contributing to the effectiveness of IPE programming (Cahn et al., 2016; Frye & Hemmer, 2012; Thistlethwaite et al., 2015). IPCP has generally been assumed to be an effective practice strategy to improve patient outcomes and realize the goals of the Quadruple Aim, and logically IPE would be the appropriate mechanism to drive this shift in healthcare. However, there are gaps in the literature regarding the ultimate effectiveness of pre-professional IPE—namely, does it indeed prove patient outcomes (Cox et al., 2016)? Cahn et al. (2016) posit that it is difficult determine the effect of pre-professional IPE on clinical outcomes due to the number of confounding factors contributing to clinical performance and practice behaviors after students graduate. Indeed, it has been suggested that the way to determine if IPE is effective at improving patient outcomes is to shift the focus of evaluation to that of professional IPE that is incorporated into the work setting of licensed professionals (Cox et al., 2016). The question that logically follows is, what should be measured to demonstrate effectiveness of pre-professional (pre-licensure) IPE?

BACKGROUND AND CONTEXT

Assessment and evaluation in pre-professional IPE is widely discussed among educators in the field. Most of the existing literature on IPE assessment includes reports of specific activities, rather than longitudinal program evaluation. These assessments most often consist of outcomes at the learner reaction level (attitudes and opinions of students most commonly), and the data are usually the result of a student self-report mechanism like a questionnaire (Blue et al., 2015; Kahaleh et al., 2015; Reeves et al., 2015; Thistlethwaite et al., 2015). Additionally, the assessments are typically completed as soon as the learning activity is finished, and therefore are short-term outcome measurements (Thistlethwaite et al., 2015). Pre- to post-activity score comparison is quite common (Blue et al., 2015; Cox et al., 2016; Reeves et al., 2017; Thistlethwaite et al., 2015), and there are a variety of validated scales for assessing student attitudes and opinions toward interprofessional work (Blue et al., 2015). It appears that this type of programming is generally well-received by learners, and usually demonstrates improvements in these short-term positive learner outcomes (Reeves et al., 2017).

Shortcomings of the current literature regarding IPE assessment and evaluation include inability to draw conclusions about efficacy of IPE across the field due to heterogeneity of programming (Cox et al., 2016; McNaughton, 2017; Thistlethwaite, 2012); lack of grounding in theoretical foundation (Abu-Rish et al., 2012; Blue et al., 2015); a dearth of longitudinal studies (Abu-Rish et al., 2012; Forman et al., 2016; Thistlethwaite et al., 2015); and lack of behavioral-based assessment (Blue et al., 2015; Cox et al., 2016). Reports regarding evaluation and assessment in IPE have made several recommendations as to the types of studies needed to broaden our understanding of effective IPE programming. Recent literature calls for robust evaluation programs which consider the entirety of IPE programs at individual institutions (E. Anderson et al., 2016) rather than the individual activities that contribute to the whole. The goal of evaluating the IPE program in its totality is to understand the sum of the parts, and ultimately how well each piece works and fits within the whole to provide students with adequate preparation. It is recommended that these evaluations rest on a theoretical framework (Abu-Rish et al., 2012; Blue et al., 2015), engage multiple stakeholder groups (E. S. Anderson, 2016; Reeves et al., 2015; Thistlethwaite et al., 2015), consider institutional context (Cahn et al., 2016; Forman et al., 2016; Frye & Hemmer, 2012; Thistlethwaite et al., 2015), and utilize mixed-methods approaches (E. Anderson et al., 2016; Cahn et al., 2016; Reeves et al., 2017).

The purpose of this study was to conduct strategic inquiry in the IPE program at Pacific University to understand the strengths, weaknesses, and effectiveness of the IPE program, with the ultimate goal of improving teaching and learning in the IPE program. Pacific University enrolls approximately 1860 undergraduate and 1960 graduate students. The majority of the graduate students are students in the College of Health Professions, which is home to nine allied health professional programs. The college's commitment to excellence in IPE is evidenced by its inclusion in the strategic plan, budgetary allocations, and the dedication of specific faculty and staff positions.

METHODS

The project combined several of the above-mentioned strategies to engage multiple stakeholder groups through two cycles of data collection to provide feedback and insight about the IPE program. The project utilized a mixed methods approach, collecting both qualitative and quantitative data in cycle 1, and rested on realist evaluation as its theoretical framework (Pawson & Tilley, 1997). The results of two cycles of data collection informed the development of a redesigned foundational IPE curriculum as well as comprehensive evaluation plan for the IPE program.

Action research is "a systematic approach to investigation that enables people to find effective solutions to problems they confront in their everyday lives" (Stringer, 2014). Action research has also been described as a participatory process aimed at gaining knowledge to practically address issues of concern and provide solutions to problems (Brydon-Miller et al., 2003). Action research utilizes a cyclical process, in which the first cycle of data collection and analysis informs the later cycles of data collection and analysis, and ultimate action steps.

Participants

Cycle 1 consisted of two data collection phases—phase 1 utilized focus groups and phase 2 utilized an anonymous survey. Focus groups (Morgan, 2008) were used for the first phase of data collection. A total of five focus groups were conducted—two focus groups with faculty members and three with students. There were 11 faculty participants and 13 student participants, for a total of 24 participants in this cycle of data collection. Inclusion criteria for students were that they had to be in at least their second year of study at the College of Health Professions to ensure previous participation in the IPE program. All faculty members in the College of Health Professions were invited to participate, and only one participant did not have previous experience in the IPE program. Ethical approval was granted through Northeastern University's Institutional Review Board in accordance with the Doctor of Education program's requirements.

In phase 2, the researcher conducted a cross-sectional, anonymous survey of graduates of the College of Health Professions to determine how the pre-professional interprofessional education (IPE) program at Pacific University impacted their professional practices. Inclusion criteria for participating in the survey specified that only graduates from the previous three years (classes of 2017, 2018, and 2019) could participate, and that participants were at least 18 years old. There were several reasons for choosing these inclusion criteria: in the first three years after graduation, it is more likely that the university would have valid email addresses for the graduates; participants should still be new enough in the field and closer in time to their graduation date to have fresher perceptions regarding their pre-professional training; and limiting to the previous three years of graduates should reduce the confounding factor of interprofessional training delivered on the job while still capturing enough time for graduates to have adjusted to professional work and to have developed a good understanding of the level at which their pre-professional training prepared them.

Data Collection

This action research study utilized a mixed methods approach. For Cycle 1, the researcher conducted focus groups with students and faculty members to understand their teaching and learning experiences in the IPE program, as well as their perceptions of areas for improvement, growth, and change. Focus group protocols (Jacob & Furgerson, 2012) were used to facilitate the sessions. There were main questions in the protocol (Rubin & Rubin, 2018), and follow up questions were improvised during the focus groups. Each session was audio recorded and the recordings were sent to www.rev.com for transcription. Transcripts were verified for accuracy using the audio recordings.

After completion of focus group analyses, the researcher conducted an anonymous survey of graduates to better understand the most and least helpful parts of the IPE program in preparing them for clinical work, as well as to gather data regarding the interprofessional nature of their current workplaces. There were 1,580 graduates of the College of Health Professions from the classes of 2017, 2018, and 2019. Sample size calculation determined that 168 completed surveys would be needed to achieve statistical power (assuming 7% margin of error, 95% confidence interval). Because response rates are often low with survey research, a census approach (Muijs, 2011) was used in which the survey was sent to the entire population (all graduates from 2017, 2018, and 2019) to improved chances that statistical power would be met.

Data Analysis

In cycle 1, a manual thematic coding approach was utilized to analyze the data from the focus group phase. NVivo (QSR International) was used to facilitate this process. A first pass review identified codes relevant to the research questions (Auerbach & Silverstein, 2003) resulting in an initial list containing 35 codes. This list was then condensed into a more concise set of 15 codes with operational definitions. This final set of codes was applied for the second pass analysis of the transcripts, grouping repeating ideas identified by this set of codes (Auerbach & Silverstein, 2003). This second analysis facilitated derivation of four final themes to which all codes could be linked. After the analysis, a visual display of the data was developed (Figure 7.1).

Descriptive and inferential statistical analyses of the graduate survey were completed using SPSS.

Action Research Process

This combination of data derived in cycle 1 informed the actions steps in cycle 2—the development of an improved foundational IPE curriculum and comprehensive evaluation plan for the IPE program. Engaging students, faculty members, and graduates in this strategic inquiry for improvement welcomed those who were actively involved in delivering and receiving education in this program in the process of informing change—the central goal of action research.

The literature and data analysis from Cycle 1 informed the need for an improvement plan as well as specific program elements that needed to be addressed. The primary working team that completed action step activities included the researcher and course leads for the foundational interprofessional competence course (IPC). They collaborated over the course of several months using regular working meetings to develop the revised foundational program curriculum which incorporates foundational learning in diversity, equity, and inclusion with learning about the IPEC competencies for interprofessional practice. This curricular transformation brought the original 4-week long IPC course to an 8-week long course, now called *Foundations for Interprofessional Practice, Equity, and Inclusion* (FIP). They also suggested and justified a shift to make the interprofessional case conference series (ICC) optional to improve student buy in for that learning activity (two ICC style case discussions have been embedded into the new foundational curriculum to replace the required attendance at two ICCs, and the students will be able to complete these activities with their established IP team from the FIP course). Lastly, they worked together to establish a comprehensive program evaluation plan to evaluate the IPE program in its entirety, including bi-annual focus groups with faculty and students; a bi-annual cost-benefit analysis; bi-annual graduate surveys; and annual analyses of faculty scores of student performance. All action steps were taken collaboratively and the team incorporated regular updates and requests for guidance and feedback from the Dean of the College of Health Professions as well as the university-level Interprofessional Education Steering Committee (IPESC).

The evaluation for the cycle 2 action steps consisted of a manual thematic analysis of field notes from all meetings, monthly analytic memos, and data from an evaluation focus group with the other Associate Dean and foundational course co-coordinators. NVivo was again used to facilitate the analysis.

Trustworthiness and Quality Assurance

Reflexivity was used throughout the study to maintain confirmability. As part of every fieldnote, there is a reflective portion in which the researcher's impact on process and product were documented. Additionally, the feelings and impressions of the researcher were captured here and these two elements provided a nice frame for examining bias and how the researcher's views impacted the work (Lincoln & Guba, 1985). Regarding the analysis process, source triangulation (comparing feedback from the student focus groups and faculty focus groups) and member checking were utilized to establish credibility (Lincoln & Guba, 1985). Additionally, triangulation of data and reflexivity were used to establish confirmability. Thick description was used in qualitative analyses to support transferability and to help provide adequate context for understanding the themes derived from data collection. All fieldnotes and analytic memos were shared with the dissertation chair throughout cycle 2, providing an avenue for external review and establishing dependability.

FINDINGS

Cycle 1 Findings

There were significant areas of overlap in student and faculty perceptions, and this triangulation of sources provided confidence in the findings. The main themes from the findings were buy-in, relevance, value, and program content/structure. Students identified issues of buy-in related to whether or not IP learning activities were required or voluntary in nature. Additionally, faculty members identified issues of buy-in stemming from department leadership, faculty recognition, and general interest in IP work. Relevance emerged as the second theme identified by both student and faculty focus groups. Students and faculty agreed that some of the IP activities can seem unrealistic because of the number of professions that participate and the lack of real-world communication and work barriers posed in the premise. Both student and faculty focus groups addressed value, or "bang-for-your-buck," with regard to IP activities. Most participants felt that applied learning activities were the most meaningful experiences, specifically citing clinical practice and applied, case-based learning type activities. Program content and structure emerged as the last major theme, in which lack of work requirements or deliverables led to low enthusiasm, as well as the suggestion that longitudinal programming or more experiences with established IP teams would be valuable. Finally, students and faculty agreed that the IPE program would benefit from more content in social justice, diversity, equity, and inclusion, and that faculty development would be needed to prepare facilitators to deliver this content. Figure 7.1 is a data display from the cycle 1 faculty and student focus groups.

Completed surveys were received from 113 individuals (response rate 10%), which did not reach threshold indicated by power calculation, indicating that results should be interpreted with caution. The primary findings from the graduate survey about pre-professional IPE training provided confirmation of themes derived from the cycle 1 focus groups. Ninety percent of participants agreed or strongly agreed that they were well-prepared for IPCP upon graduation (n=100). Ninety-six participants answered the question asking which IPE activities were most useful. Of those, 63% (n=60) identified clinical interprofessional education experiences as the most useful, while 34% (n=33) identified case-based learning as the most effective. Regarding attitudes towards team-based care, 100% agreed or strongly agreed that the interprofessional approach improves the quality of care

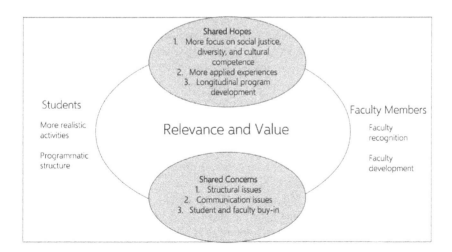

FIGURE 7.1. Faculty and Student Focus Group Findings

to patients/clients (n=113); and 96% agreed or strongly agreed that developing a patient/client care plan with other team members avoids errors in delivering care.

Kruskal-Wallis analysis (with Bonferroni correction) indicated that significant differences in rates of IPCP existed between professions ($p<.001$). Follow up pairwise comparisons demonstrated that dental hygienists participated at significantly lower rates than occupational therapists ($p=.006$), physician assistants ($p=.016$), and psychologists ($p=.003$). Kruskal-Wallis analysis (with Bonferroni correction) indicated that significant differences in rates of IPCP existed between organizational models ($p<.001$). Follow up pairwise comparisons demonstrated that patient-centered medical homes fostered IPCP at higher rates than solo private practices ($p=.026$), and that coordinated care organizations fostered higher rates than solo private practices ($p<.001$). There were no significant differences in levels of perceived preparedness for IPCP when participants were compared by year of graduation, or between those who earned the concentration in IPE and those who did not.

Cycle 2 Findings

There were four primary findings from the evaluation of cycle 2 action steps. The findings were that the collaborative process was key to success; that stakeholder engagement was critical to the process; that the iterative process of action research facilitated a strong process and quality work products; and that the value of this work was widely appreciated.

Collaborative Leadership

This project embedded principles of collaborative leadership, and the action steps were completed in collaboration with others. When asked what made the action steps processes effective, collaborators cited clear communication and teamwork as a key element of project success. Relationship building was also identified as a contributing element to the collaborative approach and success of the project. Additionally, text from fieldnotes and analytic memos also speak to the importance of collaboration and relationship building as facilitators for a strong work process and development of good work products.

Stakeholder Engagement

The critical nature of stakeholder engagement also emerged as a finding from the evaluation of cycle 2 action steps. It was crucial to engage others in different roles to understand their perspectives as well as to incorporate needed expertise that the researcher did not have. There are several examples of this. First was that the researcher did not have the necessary experience in diversity, equity, and inclusion (DEI) to lead the development of the new foundational curriculum. Additionally, administrator feedback shaped the development of the project and highlighted areas of consideration from the administrative standpoint.

Iterative Process

The iterative process of action research also emerged as a key driver of success in this dissertation in practice project. The entire action step process was a series of working meetings, collecting regular feedback, incorporating that feedback, and moving forward in light of stakeholders' thoughts, opinions, and expertise. The continual integration of feedback was lauded by participating collaborators and facilitated a research- and stakeholder-informed process to develop the curriculum plan for the revised IPC course as well as the comprehensive evaluation plan. When asked about what aspects of the action step processes were particularly effective, the iterative process was mentioned several times.

Value of Project

The fourth main finding from cycle 2 evaluation was that the nature of the work (incorporating foundational DEI learning into our required IPC course) has been very meaningful and needed at the university. There were many comments in meetings throughout the year (noted in fieldnotes) about the value of the work being done and appreciation that the researcher and collaborators were working to make needed changes. The value of this work also showed up in comments, specifically from the administration, about meeting strategic plan goals for accreditation. The timing of the action steps for this dissertation in practice was in alignment with wide calls for social justice that were issued in the wake of George Floyd's murder. The cycle 1 finding that students and faculty both felt improvements and increases in DEI curriculum for the IPE program were needed was then confirmed by student calls for action in May and June of 2020. That drove support for the course development and wide buy-in for the 8-week curricular model which was ultimately approved. There was wide recognition that this type of curricular development was needed, which facilitated a smooth action step process. Figure 7.2 is a data display from the cycle 2 evaluation.

DISCUSSION

Collaborative Leadership Drove Success

This research utilized stakeholder feedback to understand the current state of the IPE program and to develop a revised foundational curriculum and comprehensive evaluation plan to understand the ultimate impacts of those changes. This project embraced the principles of collaborative leadership in working towards implementing change at the university. Collaborative leadership is "the process of engaging collective intelligence to deliver results across organizational boundaries when ordinary mechanisms of control are absent" (Hurley, 2011). The concept of collaborative leadership rests on the idea that pooled intelligence and effort leads to better outcomes than when change efforts are led by a single individual. Collaborative leadership relies on an environment of trust, mutual respect, and shared aspiration (Hurley, 2011). The researcher utilized collaborative leadership

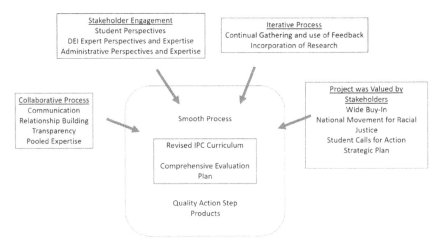

FIGURE 7.2. Cycle 2 Evaluation Findings

principles for this dissertation in practice project for several reasons: this change initiative stood to affect all students in the College of Health Professions, as well as a smaller number of students from the other colleges; the researcher felt other perspectives were needed to facilitate the work as her expertise was limited in some areas; and that it was important to center the experience, beliefs, and goals of the foundational course coordinators as the course leads who would be implementing the new curriculum.

The collaborators who participated in the evaluation focus group specifically said that this collaboration and relationship building was important for the success of the project. This is consistent with literature on collaborative leadership. It has been suggested that leadership is not about leaders—it is the practice of inviting participants to work together to create processes and move toward shared outcomes (Raelin, 2016). Indeed, it has been argued that the four most important words in leadership are "What do you think?" (Pearce & Wassenaar, 2014). The participants commented on how the researcher brought humility to the work, incorporated feedback, and focused on honoring the input of the collaborators. These processes embody the principles of collaborative leadership and built an environment of trust and mutual respect that facilitated a good work process and excellent work products.

Additionally, using a participatory process for facilitating change that benefits the majority rather than the minority is supported by the literature (Burnes et al., 2018). Involving those who will be recipients of change in the change planning process improves readiness for the change and appreciation for the long term goals (Burnes et al., 2018). Because the foundational course coordinators would ultimately be responsible for implementing the new curriculum and managing portions of the evaluation process, it was very important to include them as key players in development of the new curriculum and comprehensive evaluation plan. Lastly, the literature supports that shared leadership builds institutional memory and ownership of projects, as well as capitalizes on the expertise of many, providing a greater ability to problem solve and plan (Kezar & Holcombe, 2017).

Stakeholder Engagement was Critical

The importance of stakeholder engagement to project success was key in several areas—notably that the researcher needed to rely on the expertise of others; that it was critical to understand the students' perspectives; and that including stakeholders in the development of curriculum and the evaluation plan was important for success. Stakeholder engagement is supported by the literature in all three of these areas.

Kezar and Holcombe discuss the principles of shared leadership and particularly call out the importance of engaging individuals with relevant expertise (Kezar & Holcombe, 2017). For this project, one of the central ideas was embedding foundational learning in diversity, equity, and inclusion into the existing curriculum which focused on the IPEC competencies for interprofessional practice. One of the foundational course coordinators had significant experience in teaching DEI principles specifically as they relate to healthcare. The foundational course coordinator led the development of the curricular model for the new foundational course. Her depth of experience was critically important for bringing the curriculum together.

The engagement of stakeholders was also very important in understanding the students' experiences and perspectives. The researcher came into this project with ideas about what types of changes were needed in the IPE program. However, the student focus groups revealed that the researcher's assumptions about what was effective were not always correct. Specifically, the researcher assumed that the ICC series was an engaging and effective activity and was surprised to learn that the students in the focus groups felt that this was the least effective activity. Some of the reasons they listed were that participation was mandatory, that there were no deliverables or assessments involved, and that trying to work with a group where previous team development has not happened is challenging. The research of Rogers et al. supports the fact that including assessment in IPE programming may improve focus and buy-in (Rogers et al., 2017). Additionally, the students' feedback in focus groups supported the incorporation of DEI principles into the redesigned foundational curriculum. Students were arguably the most important stakeholder group in this situation as the consumers of education, so their inclusion in the data collection and planning efforts of this study was necessary.

Finally, the inclusion of stakeholders in the development of curriculum and the comprehensive evaluation plan is supported by recommended best practices in the literature (E. S. Anderson, 2016; Reeves & Barr, 2016; Thistlethwaite et al., 2015). One of the primary challenges faced by the IPE field is the fact that institutional context shapes and drives the development of curriculum, planning, and assessment at each institution. Because every institution has its own set of resources, challenges, and unique combination of professions, the institutional context is a key driver of how well the programming works. A thorough understanding of institutional context in the light of program planning and evaluation is important as that helps administrators understand *why* the program is functioning well or not (Olson & Bialocerkowski, 2014; Thistlethwaite, 2012). To really understand the institutional context, it was necessary for the researcher to work with stakeholders to understand their perspectives, their experiences, and their hopes for change.

The Iterative Process was Key for Success

The third finding from this project was that the use of an iterative process was very important. Participants in the evaluation focus group specifically spoke to the use of an iterative process and continual collection and incorporation of feedback as being key drivers of success for the initiative. The iterative process was useful in several ways: it helped deepen the understanding of institutional context; it continually incorporated feedback from stakeholders for planning purposes; and when used as a method for planning and revising the plan, the use of an iterative process operationalized the work of collaborative leadership and stakeholder engagement.

The iterative process is a hallmark of action research, in which cycles of data collection drive planning and action in an attempt to address problems of practice (Herr & Anderson, 2015). The data collected in cycle 1 drove decisions about plans in the action step process. Additionally, continual collection and use of feedback during the action step phase facilitated refinement and systematic consideration of input for the change process. The cycles of research and planning consistent with the action research model are supported by organizational change literature. Burnes presents the ideas of approaching change with an interdisciplinary team, combining efforts of leadership and management, and utilization of an action research approach (Burnes et al., 2018).

The iterative process also deepened the understanding of institutional context through the continual process of presenting plans, collecting feedback, and adjusting the plans in response to that feedback. Throughout this project, the researcher provided regular updates to the dean of the College of Health Professions as well as the Interprofessional Education Steering Committee (IPESC). Additionally, any suggestions for plans that originated with the researcher were brought to the key collaborator group, and plans were sent out for input from stakeholder groups. This process of continual revision, which was driven by stakeholders, ultimately led to solid work products in the form of the revised curriculum and comprehensive evaluation plan.

Wide Buy-In and Shared Goals made for a Smooth Process

The last finding from this project was that the shared goals and wide buy-in for the initiative paved the way for a smooth implementation process. There was a marked consistency among student and faculty feedback in the cycle 1 focus groups around the need for increasing curricular content in diversity, equity, and inclusion in the IPE program. Additionally, the murder of George Floyd in May 2020 immediately preceded the implementation of action steps for this project. As a result of his murder, as well as the violent deaths of other Black individuals, there was a wide call for action from students and faculty for the university to improve willingness to address systemic racism through curricular improvements and faculty and staff development. Increasing work in DEI was also a part of the strategic plan at the university. What this meant for the project was that all administrative groups and collaborators shared the goal of improving the program by adding this type of curriculum, and that shared buy-in for progress smoothed approval processes.

The researcher's fieldnotes repeatedly reference the fact that encouragement to pursue this change was present from administrators, the IPESC, and collaborators. In his guidance on leading change, John Kotter includes the importance of developing a shared vision and strategy and establishing a sense of urgency as keys for successful organizational transformation (Kotter, 1996). In this project, the shared vision and goals were evident as a result of the national movement for racial justice, as well as earlier feedback from students and faculty that more time and work was needed in this area. This shared value and wide buy-in contributed to a smooth process—at no point did the project hit a roadblock with approvals, despite the increased cost of delivering the new curriculum.

LIMITATIONS

The main limitations of this study include potential response bias and limited generalizability. Specifically, those who are more interested in the IPE program were probably more likely to respond to the recruitment messages than those who may feel less favorably about the program. There were insufficient responses to the graduate survey to reach statistical power, so the ability to draw conclusions from the resulting data are limited.

Additionally, because the study addressed the IPE program at Pacific University specifically, the individual context of the institution is incredibly important in understanding the study findings themselves and broad generalizability may be limited. However, the themes derived from the cycle 1 and 2 data analyses are reflected in other studies in IPE literature, which supports generalizability beyond the institution to other IPE programs.

IMPLICATIONS FOR PRACTICE

The implications for practice stemming from this study emphasize the importance of stakeholder engagement and collaborative processes when evaluating program efficacy and pursuing changes such as program improvement. The success of this project was largely due to the inclusion of critical voices and the intentionality of understanding different perspectives from those who had participated in the IPE program.

Research supports the use of collaborative approaches in change management. The experience for the researcher and stakeholders involved in this project are concurrent with those findings. Additionally, the IPE literature supports stakeholder engagement and collaboration in planning and implementing comprehensive program evaluations in IPE. The action research methodology utilized in this study resulted in quality outcomes and a process that was valued and respected by participants.

Educators and administrators at other institutions should consider the use of action research methodologies and the implementation of collaborative leadership principles in engaging in planned program evaluation and change projects. These approaches proved to facilitate a rich work process while simultaneously centering the concerns of stakeholders and program users. Additionally, stakeholder engagement and collaborative leadership principles increased the understanding of the institutional context which shapes the IPE program. In conclusion, reliance on best practices supported by IPE literature and adherence to the principles of collaborative leadership and action research resulted in a successful work process and quality work products.

REFERENCES

Abu-Rish, E., Kim, S., Choe, L., Varpio, L., Malik, E., White, A. A., Craddick, K., Blondon, K., Robins, L., Nagasawa, P., Thigpen, A., Chen, L. L., Rich, J., & Zierler, B. (2012). Current trends in interprofessional education of health sciences students: A literature review. *Journal of Interprofessional Care*, *26*(6), 444–451. https://doi.org/10.3109/13561820.2012.715604

Anderson, E. S. (2016). Evaluating interprofessional education: An important step to improving practice and influencing policy. *Journal of Taibah University Medical Sciences*, *11*(6), 571–578. https://doi.org/10.1016/j.jtumed.2016.08.012

Anderson, E., Smith, R., & Hammick, M. (2016). Evaluating an interprofessional education curriculum: A theory-informed approach. *Medical Teacher*, *38*(4), 385–394. https://doi.org/10.3109/0142159X.2015.1047756

Auerbach, C. F., & Silverstein, L. B. (2003). *Qualitative data: An introduction to coding and analysis*. New York University Press.

Beasley, C. (2009). The triple aim: Optimizing health, care, and cost. *Healthcare Executive*, *24*(1), 64–65. www.ihi.org.

Blue, A. V., Chesluk, B. J., Conforti, L. N., & Holmboe, E. S. (2015). Assessment and evaluation in interprofessional education: Exploring the field. *Journal of Allied Health*, *44*(2), 73–82. http://www.ncbi.nlm.nih.gov/pubmed/26046114

Bodenheimer, T., & Sinsky, C. (2014). From triple to quadruple aim: Care of the patient requires care of the provider. *Annals of Family Medicine, 12*(6), 573–576. https://doi.org/10.1370/afm.1713.Center

Brandt, B. F. (2015). Interprofessional education and collaborative practice: Welcome to the "new" forty-year old field. *The Advisor,* 9–17.

Brydon-Miller, M., Greenwood, D., Maguire, P., & Bradbury, H. (2003). Why action research? *Action Research, 11*(11), 9–28.

Burnes, B., Hughes, M., & By, R. T. (2018). Reimagining organisational change leadership. *Leadership, 14*(2), 141–158. https://doi.org/10.1177/1742715016662188

Cahn, P. S., Bzowyckyj, A., Collins, L., Dow, A., Goodell, K., Johnson, A. F., Klocko, D., Knab, M., Parker, K., Reeves, S., & Zierler, B. K. (2016). A design thinking approach to evaluating interprofessional education. *Journal of Interprofessional Care, 30*(3), 378–380. https://doi.org/10.3109/13561820.2015.1122582

Cox, M., Cuff, P., Brandt, B., Reeves, S., & Zierler, B. (2016). Measuring the impact of interprofessional education on collaborative practice and patient outcomes. *Journal of Interprofessional Care, 30*(1), 1–3. https://doi.org/10.3109/13561820.2015.1111052

Forman, D., Jones, M., & Thistlethwaite, J. (2016). *Leading research and evaluation in interprofessional education and collaboratove practice.* Palgrave Macmillan.

Frye, A. W., & Hemmer, P. A. (2012). Program evaluation models and related theories: AMEE Guide No. 67. *Medical Teacher, 34*(5). https://doi.org/10.3109/0142159X.2012.668637

Health Professions Accreditors Collaborative. (2019). *Guidance on developing quality interprofessional education for the health professions.* Health Professions Accreditors Collaborative.

Herr, K., & Anderson, G. (2015). *The action research dissertation: A guide for students and faculty* (2nd ed.). Sage Publications.

Hurley, T. J. (2011). Collaborative leadership: engaging collective intelligence to acheive results across organisational boundaries. *Oxford Leadership, October.* https://www.oxfordleadership.com/wp-content/uploads/2022/09/oxford-leadership-collaborative-leadership.pdf

Jacob, S. a S., & Furgerson, S. P. (2012). Writing interview protocols and conducting interviews : Tips for students new to the field of qualitative research. *The Qualitative Report, 17*(42), 1–10. https://doi.org/; http://www.nova.edu/ssss/QR/QR17/jacob.pdf

Kahaleh, A. A., Danielson, J., Franson, K. L., Nuffer, W. A., & Umland, E. M. (2015). An interprofessional education panel on development, implementation, and assessment strategies. *American Journal of Pharmaceutical Education, 79*(6), 1–10. https://doi.org/10.5688/ajpe79678

Kezar, A., & Holcombe, E. (2017). *Shared leadership in higher education: Important lessons from research and practice* (pp. 1–29). American Council on Education.

Kotter, J. (1996). *Leading change.* Harvard Business School Press.

Lapkin, S., Levett-Jones, T., & Gilligan, C. (2013). A systematic review of the effectiveness of interprofessional education in health professional programs. *Nurse Education Today.* https://doi.org/10.1016/j.nedt.2011.11.006

Lincoln, Y., & Guba, E. (1985). *Naturalistic inquiry.* Sage Publications.

McNaughton, S. (2017). The long-term impact of undergraduate interprofessional education on graduate interprofessional practice: A scoping review. *Journal of Interprofessional Care*, *32*(4), 1–10. https://doi.org/10.1080/13561820.2017.1417239

Morgan, D. L. (2008). Focus groups. In *The Sage encyclopedia of qualitative research methods* (pp. 353–354). https://doi.org/10.5860/rusq.49n1.101

Muijs, D. (2011). *Doing quantitative research in education with SPSS* (2nd ed.). Sage Publications.

Olson, R., & Bialocerkowski, A. (2014). Interprofessional education in allied health: A systematic review. *Medical Education*. https://doi.org/10.1111/medu.12290

Pawson, R., & Tilley, N. (1997). An introduction to scientific realist evaluation. In E. Chelimsky & W. R. Shadish (Eds.), *Evaluation for the 21st century: A handbook* (pp. 405–418). Sage Publications, Inc. https://doi.org/10.4135/9781483348896.n29

Pearce, C. L., & Wassenaar, C. L. (2014). Leadership is like fine wine: It is meant to be shared, globally. *Organizational Dynamics*, *43*(1), 9–16. https://doi.org/10.1016/j.orgdyn.2013.10.002

Raelin, J. A. (2016). It's not about the leaders. *Organizational Dynamics*, *45*(2), 124–131. https://doi.org/10.1016/j.orgdyn.2016.02.006

Reeves, S., & Barr, H. (2016). Twelve steps to evaluating interprofessional education. *Journal of Taibah University Medical Sciences*, *11*(6), 601–605. https://doi.org/10.1016/j.jtumed.2016.10.012

Reeves, S., Boet, S., Zierler, B., & Kitto, S. (2015). Interprofessional education and practice guide No. 3: Evaluating interprofessional education. *Journal of Interprofessional Care*, *29*(4), 305–312. https://doi.org/10.3109/13561820.2014.1003637

Reeves, S., Palaganas, J., & Zierler, B. (2017). An updated synthesis of review evidence of interprofessional education. *Journal of Allied Health*, *46*(1), 56–61.

Rogers, G. D., Thistlethwaite, J. E., Anderson, E. S., Abrandt Dahlgren, M., Grymonpre, R. E., Moran, M., & Samarasekera, D. D. (2017). International consensus statement on the assessment of interprofessional learning outcomes. *Medical Teacher*, *39*(4), 347–359. https://doi.org/10.1080/0142159X.2017.1270441

Rubin, B. H. J., & Rubin, I. S. (2018). *Structuring the Interview*. Sage Publications.

Stringer, E. (2014). *Action research* (4th ed.). Sage Publications.

Thistlethwaite, J. (2012). Interprofessional education: A review of context, learning and the research agenda. *Medical Education*. https://doi.org/10.1111/j.1365-2923.2011.04143.x

Thistlethwaite, J., Kumar, K., Moran, M., Saunders, R., & Carr, S. (2015). An exploratory review of pre-qualification interprofessional education evaluations. *Journal of Interprofessional Care*, *29*(4). https://doi.org/10.3109/13561820.2014.985292

World Health Organization. (2010). Framework for action on interprofessional education & collaborative practice. In *Practice*. https://doi.org/10.1111/j.1741-1130.2007.00144.x

CHAPTER 8

CREATING AND USING A CAREER DEVELOPMENT COURSE TO PREPARE LIFE SCIENCE STUDENTS FOR CAREER DECISION MAKING

Serena L. Christianson and Ray R. Buss

INTRODUCTION

"What do you want to be when you grow up?" Practically every child has been asked this question, inspiring excitement initially and panic frequently when they are young adults. Throughout their early education, students were introduced to a limited buffet of career options: teaching, law, public safety (firefighter/police officer), healthcare, engineering, trade careers, and military service. If high school graduates pursued college, the question advanced to "What are you majoring in?" The paradox of these questions was that students "don't know what they don't know" in terms of career options, yet they have been expected to select their careers with little or no knowledge about careers or career options, the *problem of practice* (PoP) leading to these studies. Further, students often felt obligated to

Faculty Development: Achieving Change Through Action Research, pages 111–125.
Copyright © 2024 by Information Age Publishing
www.infoagepub.com
All rights of reproduction in any form reserved.

select financially stable and secure career pathways. They have been bombarded with messages about lucrative, desirable jobs, which were commonly categorized under the STEM (science, technology, engineering, and mathematics) umbrella.

Throughout the 21st century, national policymakers and scientists have focused on raising awareness about the opportunities in STEM. From 2009 to 2015, "Employment in STEM occupations grew by 10.5 percent … compared with 5.2 percent net growth in non-STEM occupations" (Fayer et al., 2017, p. 2). Moreover, "STEM occupations are projected to grow by 8.9 percent from 2014 to 2024, compared to 6.4 percent growth for non-STEM occupations" (Noonan, 2017, p. 2).

Despite this need for and persuasive efforts to advance careers in the sciences, if asked what sorts of jobs were possible in STEM, many STEM students' answers, particularly those in the life sciences, typically fell into one of two categories: research or medicine. Students simply have been unaware they could become beekeepers, forest planners, genetic counselors, science illustrators, veterinarians, videographers, winery microbiologists, among other life science career pathways.

In this chapter, we have described two action research studies, designed and implemented to provide career development for life science students. Specifically, the purpose of this project was to provide job/career information to ensure School of Life Sciences (SOLS) students had appropriate, comprehensive information as they learned about career exploration and considered life sciences career opportunities.

BACKGROUND AND CONTEXT

Providing adequate resources for undergraduate students' career development has been important to meet demands from national agencies and industry leaders who have insisted individuals possess STEM skills. SOLS students have not always attained the position they initially desired; thus, students' consideration of alternative career paths has become more important to use their degree in more flexible ways. By offering a career development course in SOLS, students' awareness of their options could be increased.

The purpose of this project was to provide career information to SOLS' students to ensure they were prepared for various life sciences career opportunities. The conduct of the research study was guided by two research questions. The first was, "With respect to career exploration, how did participation in a life science career development course affect students' abilities to select goals, identify occupational information, formulate action plans, conduct problem solving, and engage in self-appraisal?" The second was, "How did a life science career development course affect students' employment-seeking skills, professional and career goals, and career problem-solving and decision making abilities?"

In the next sections, we have described how three theoretical frameworks influenced the design of the work including the intervention, a life sciences career development course. Additionally, we have discussed how action research was used over serveral cycles to implement the intervention, explore its effectiveness, and make revisions to the implemenation and research processes to strengthen the work.

Holland's RIASEC Theory

John Holland (1985, 1997) created a practical typology consisting of six vocational interests including Realistic (R), Investigative (I), Artistic (A), Social (S), Enterprising (E), and Conventional (C). Use of the typology generated a three-letter code that captured individuals' primary, secondary, and tertiary career interests. Holland's RIASEC theory has been regarded as one of the premier career theories and assessments (Kennelly et al., 2018). Because of the practicality of this career theory, Holland's RIASEC theory provided a relevant approach for working with students who were examining career alternatives. Following an online assessment using Holland's RIASEC framework, students used the information to aid their exploration of careers and development of skills relevant to career interests.

Sampson, Peterson, Reardon, and Lenz's Cognitive Information Processing (CIP) Career Decision Theory

Sampson and his colleagues developed an approach to delivering career services to help individuals learn about the vast career opportunities in the job market, as well as teach them how to prepare for the job search process (Sampson et al., 2004). Key elements of this cognitive information processing (CIP) approach included screening individuals to determine what services were appropriate, matching staff assistance based on levels of career readiness, and using the appropriate career theory to determine the amount and type of career development service required. As part of the CIP approach, Sampson and colleagues used a triangle/pyramid configuration that served as a visual and sequential model for information processing with three distinct levels involving four components (Sampson et al., 2004, 2020). These four components focus on self-knowledge, knowledge about options, decision-making, and an executive processing domain or "thinking about thinking" (Reardon & Lenz, 2015, p. 85). See Figure 1.

Bandura's Self-Efficacy Framework

Albert Bandura (1986, 1997) has developed and refined *self-efficacy*, which was based on individuals' assessment of their ability to carry out behaviors necessary to attain certain levels of performance. Self-efficacy has been reflected in individuals' confidence and perceived ability to perform a task such as, for example, engage in career search efforts. Moreover, he cogently argued these beliefs shaped subsequent efforts and decisions. Bandura asserted that self-efficacy was influenced by four sources of information that included personal performance accomplishments or mastery experiences, vicarious learning, social persuasion, and physiological states and reactions.

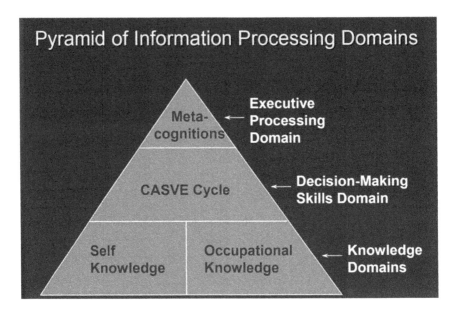

FIGURE 8.1. The Cognitive Information Processing Theory's Pyramid of Information Processing Domains based on the work of Peterson et al., 2003. Used by permission.

Of the four sources of information affecting self-efficacy, mastery experiences were the most relevant and applicable in this research context. Bandura claimed mastery experiences were the most powerful way to improve individuals' self-efficacy (Bandura, 1986, 1997). Simply stated, repeated *and* successful practices of a skill/task/behavior increased self-efficacy. The concept of "success" in this scenario referred to improving skills related to career development and exploration processes. Through such repeated behavior, confidence was developed because individuals realized they had the ability to do something like finding realistic career options.

Action Research and Its Role in the Project

Action Research (AR) was well suited to the current study for several reasons. First, the problem of practice, a local issue of providing more options for students through career information and career exploration, was embedded in the first author's workplace context. Second, teachers and other educators have effectively used AR in various contexts to solve local problems/issues. Third, a small, purposive sample was available to participate in the study. Fourth, researcher developed instruments such as interviews and a class assignment were employed to gather data on the effectiveness of the career information and exploration program.

Consistent with the typical application of AR, the first author executed the AR four-step process across a number of cycles. The four-step process included (a) studying and planning, (b) taking action, (c) collecting and analyzing data, and (d) reflecting on the data to determine next steps (Mertler, 2017). In the current study, these steps were executed over two cycles to enhance the work and its results.

Implications

Taken together, there are several implications for the AR work. For the intervention, providing instruction in skills and processes related to career choice seems like a viable way to teach students to analyze the suitability of career paths through course activities involving introspection, exploration, analysis, synthesis, and planning. This intentional and repeated practice of career exploration and analysis will give students a better sense of their strengths, knowledge, skills, and potential; and help students to expand their views of possible career options and enhance self-efficacy to use these processes.

METHODS

ASU's School of Life Sciences (SOLS) served as the site where the two cycles of action research were conducted. When the AR cycles were undertaken, SOLS had over 5,200 undergraduates pursuing a variety of degrees including biological sciences, biomedical sciences, microbiology, molecular biosciences and biotechnology, and neuroscience among others. SOLS has served as an academic unit within the College of Liberal Arts and Sciences, ASU's largest academic division. This multidisciplinary School has become a leader in teaching technologies and research initiatives, demonstrating a commitment to scholarly excellence for students of all backgrounds, whether they were enrolled in face-to-face or online programs.

Participants

Brief descriptions of the participants involved in action research Cycles 1 and 2 have been provided below.

Cycle 1 Participants

Consistent with IRB requirements, participants included three student volunteers from 27 SOLS students enrolled in the course. The three students included a female, junior in biological sciences; and a female and a male, both seniors in neurobiology, physiology, and behavior.

Cycle 2 Participants

Again, consistent with IRB requirements, interview participants included eight student volunteers from the 34 enrolled in the course. Seven were seniors and one was a junior. Seven were females and one was a male. Four were from the general biological sciences major; two were from the genetics, cell, and developmental biology concentration; one was from biomedical sciences; and one was from conservation biology and ecology. Eight students also provided permission for their final essay projects to be reviewed.

Intervention

The intervention for Cycle 1, fall 2019, and Cycle 2, spring 2020, involved implementation of a 7.5-week, career information and exploration curriculum for students. In the curriculum, students were exploring their values and career-related interests, obtaining a Holland RAISEC code, conducting a career field analysis of two careers, creating a strategic plan for academic and career goals, engaging in written assignments, participating in discussion forum activities, and so on.

Data Collection

Data collection procedures varied slightly for the two action research cycles.

Cycle 1 Data Collection

A semi-structured interview consisting of nine questions was developed to assess the students' understanding of career exploration and career development and the effectiveness of the course. For example, students were asked "After taking this course, have you changed personally? If so, how? If not, why not?" Follow-up questions were asked during the interview based on the participants' responses.

Cycle 2 Data Collection

The same nine-question, semi-structured interview was used in Cycle 2. Again, follow-up questions were asked based on responses. To triangulate the results, data were also analyzed from eight students' Strategic Academic/Career Planning essay projects. In these essays, students wrote about what they learned from the class, using the CASVE—communication, analysis, synthesis, valuing, and execution—decision making cycle phases of CIP as section headers, and several reflective and analytical questions. These data served as another source to assess the effectiveness of the career development class on students' perceived career readiness, knowledge about employment-seeking skills, and career decision-making self-efficacy. Including additional data allowed us to triangulate the data and assess their support of one another. Notably, if similar conclusions were drawn from various data sources, trustworthiness of the interpretation of the results would be enhanced.

Data Analysis and Credibility of the Analysis

For Cycles 1 and 2, interview data were analyzed using Strauss and Corbin's (1998) constant comparative method at each step throughout the data analysis process. After initial coding, larger categories of codes were created, which were then aggregated into themes. The same process was used with the Strategic Academic/Career Planning project data from Cycle 2. Additionally, in Cycle 2, themes were grouped to develop assertions.

To build credibility, the first author engaged in systematic processes of coding and interpreting the qualitative data (Saldaña, 2016; Strauss & Corbin, 1998). She completed the coding and interpretive processes using careful examination and reflection at each step of the process, developing and drawing upon analytic memos to guide her efforts, and engaging in systematic processes to ensure the data supported the interpretations (Guba, 1981).

RESULTS

The results have been reported in two separate sections, one for each cycle of research.

Cycle 1 Results

The major themes derived from the Cycle 1 interviews were (a) expanding perceptions of career options, (b) increasing confidence, and (c) overwhelming support for the course.

Expanding Perceptions of Career Options

All three students were emphatic about how this course changed and expanded their perspectives of career options in the life sciences. They expressed appreciation that the course provided them with tools to explore career pathways, such as informational interviews, learning their Holland codes, and the thought and reflective processes involved in the major writing assignments. Students reflected on feeling lost and/or confused about their career options prior to the course and this course helped to provide much-needed clarity.

Increasing Confidence

Students described how they entered the course with unclear ideas about which career options to pursue and lacking confidence in how to about investigating career options. Learning about themselves and career exploration tools and resources diminished their concerns. As they were learning how to refine what their career ambitions through the course activities, they gained confidence in employing career-related search skills.

Overwhelming Support for the Course

Students were asked whether they would recommend this course to others, and each quickly responded with a definitive "yes" response. All students expressed interest in promoting this course to others because of the positive benefits they experienced. They had their own suggestions for slightly modifying the course based on personal preferences. Nevertheless, none of them indicated changes were necessary for the foundation of the course–the textbook and content, sequence of the readings, and tasks—discussion boards, readings, and assignments. All three students were very emphatic about how this course helped them find direction in their career choice.

Cycle 2 Results

Three themes were derived from the theme-related components including (a) balancing tensions relating to career choice, (b) expanding perceptions of career options, and (c) developing career exploration and planning skills. Subsequently, assertions based on the themes were developed. In Table 8.1, we have provided the theme-related components, themes, and assertions for the Cycle 2 study. See Table 8.1. Following the table, we have provided illustrative quotes to demonstrate the data and allow students' voices to be represented.

In their responses, students discussed their impending graduation and the need to make some kind of decision about their future. For example, in her final essay, Nancy (all names are pseudonyms) discussed how she was using the course to assist with both her academic and career planning when she wrote,

TABLE 8.1. Theme-Related Components, and Assertations from Cycle 2

Themes* and Theme-Related Components		Assertions
Balancing tensions relating to career choice 1. Seeking balance between financial stability and personal wellbeing 2. Alluding to the concept of socially acceptable jobs 3. Feeling pressure and urgency to make a career decision 4. Avoiding starting a job search	1.	Students enrolled in the course for reasons such as determining a career choice that met their needs and preferences while managing expectations and pressures from external sources.
Expanding perceptions of career options 1. Describing jobs believed to be available for life sciences majors 2. Appreciating discussion and practice of soft skills 3. Extending views on lifestyles	2.	Participation in this course provided a space where students were exposed to varying types of careers, applied their life science knowledge, and learned about the world of work.
Developing career exploration and planning skills 1. Appreciating resources from class and seeking their own career planning resources 2. Learning about one's values and desires 3. Showing increased confidence in oneself	3.	Engaging in the structured CASVE cycle helped students mitigate negative self-talk related to career planning and development. The intervention resources and techniques for students to conduct an effective job search campaign. The course helped develop the students' career exploration and planning skills, resulting in increased confidence and self-efficacy.

*Themes presented in italic font.

> I think what really changed it, was when my roommates started getting full-time job offers with the companies they interned for. .... Or, my other friends ... were taking the MCAT .... and I didn't want to do that .... So, I was stuck in this place where half of my friends are applying to graduate school, half of my friends are getting full-time jobs, and I'm sitting here with no plans, yet.

In her final essay, Tina discussed how the career exploration course encouraged students to engage in internships and other experiences to further define their career preferences. She realized she was at a deficit because "I do not have the experience to know if I would enjoy a career in medicine, and at the beginning of the semester, I did not know what my other options were beyond this" and she indicated the course provided information and resources to solve that difficulty.

Students discussed how participating in course assignments revealed traits and qualities that they had not realized they possessed, motivating them to treat themselves more judiciously and to trust in their capabilities. For example, during the interview, Oaklie claimed,

> I learned that I do have skills that are important, or that I've learned more through my courses than I thought I did. Not in terms of necessarily the course information, but my thought process toward problem solving and analyzing work and data.

Taken together, results indicated the career exploration course was highly effective. Further, these results provided a comprehensive picture of students' development of career search skills and determination of career options. In particular, students participated in the course to aid them in determining career choices that met their needs as they managed expectations and pressures from external sources. Additionally, students were afforded a space where they were exposed to varying types of careers, applied their life science knowledge, and learned about the world of work. Finally, the intervention introduced resources and techniques students applied to conduct an effective job search. Notably, the course helped develop the students' career exploration and planning skills, resulting in increased confidence and self-efficacy.

DISCUSSION

The discussion is presented in several sections including consistency of the studies, connections to the research literature, limitations, implications for practice, and conclusions.

Consistency of the Studies

In Cycle 2, the added collection and analysis of data from the Strategic Academic/Career Planning final essay project provides information that can be used to triangulate the data from the interviews. Specifically, the two kinds of data point to the same conclusions about the effectiveness of the intervention and its support of students' development of career search skills and exploration of career options. Notably, the results from Cycle 2 are also consistent with those from Cycle 1. Having two sets of data that support one another in this fashion attests to the efficacy of the intervention and to the development of the career search skills and understanding of career options as a result of participation in the course.

Leveraging the Action Research Process in the Studies

In the following sections, we describe how we leverage action research (AR) to attack the problem of practice (PoP) and how AR leads to the results we obtain. In particular, we discuss each step in the AR process and how we capitalize on them to design the work, implement it, gather data, and understand the outcomes.

Studying and Planning for Action Research

In the first step of an AR cycle, the researcher studies and plans the AR that will be done in that cycle. Given the PoP, no or limited understanding of careers and career options among life sciences students, the first author begins the AR process by studying the literature related to career options, career choice, and career exploration. In her work in this area, she focuses on theoretical perspectives that help her to (a) understand her PoP or those that help her to (b) develop an intervention to remedy the PoP. To understand her PoP, she selects Holland's (1985, 1997) Theory of Vocational Choice, which she uses to aid her understanding of the PoP because it shows how students can be classified into six vocational interest areas. Her choice of Holland's theory also becomes useful as she develops the intervention because she uses it as a beginning point from which students can explore career options.

With respect to an intervention to aid career exploration, the first author examines Sampson et al.'s (2004) Cognitive Information Processing (CIP) Career Decision Theory, which is applied as a way to deliver career services education so students learn skills to explore career opportunities and prepare for the job search process. The model provides a clear four component process that can be used to teach students about exploring career options and making decisions about careers.

Taking Action

In the second step of an AR cycle, the researcher implements the intervention, the action, in an attempt to remedy the PoP. To do so, the first author creates a 7.5-week, seven module course designed around the textbook *Career development & planning: A comprehensive approach* (Reardon et al., 2019). In each module, students reflect on three important concepts from the week's readings sharing their thoughts with peers in a discussion board activity.

In Module 1, chapters 1 and 2, content focuses on introducing career planning including the first domain in the CIP's Pyramid: Knowing about Myself. Other content incudes introducing the CIP Pyramid to foster students' thinking to aid their career decisions. Then, students reflect on their values, interests, and skills and develop goals related to their current and future career goals. In Module 2, chapters 3, 4, and 9, students continue the introspective, reflection process. The focus is to expand students' thinking about options for career pathways.

In Module 3, chapters 5 and 6, students continue to learn about the CIP Pyramid, transitioning into the top level, the executive processing domain. Students consider how they think about their career decisions including self-talk, self-awareness, monitoring, and control, as well as external forces influencing career paths. Module 4, chapters 11–13, focuses on how to launch an employment search campaign and the importance of written and interpersonal communications. Students also do a Career Field Analysis project, which requires them to write a brief paper after they research and reflect on two distinct occupational outlooks including salary potential, interests and skills used, work and learning conditions, and necessary training and education. In Module 5, chapters 7, 8, and 10, students return to the discussion of social conditions affecting career development, as they consider careers in the global economy, examine organizational culture and effective work, and explore career and family roles.

Modules 6 and 7, chapters 14–15, are designed and introduced together to allow students time to complete the final tasks for the course. These modules challenge students to think about life beyond the course, finding meaning in the past weeks' readings and activities, looking ahead to negotiating and evaluating job offers, and what to expect in the first phase of their careers. Finally, students complete a comprehensive reflection in the Strategic Academic/Career Planning project in which they reflect on their journey in this course.

Collecting and Analyzing Data

Interview data are gathered and analyzed as described above. We offer only several important highlights, here. For Cycle 1, interview data are analyzed using Strauss and Corbin's (1998) constant comparative method at each step of the analysis. After initial coding, larger categories of codes are created, which are then aggregated into themes. Results from Cycle 1 indicate three themes—(a) expanding perceptions of career options, (b) increasing confidence, and (c) support for the course. The same processes are used in Cycle 2 to gather and analyze interview data as well as analyzing students' Strategic Academic/Career Planning Project data. The three themes for Cycle 2 are (a) balancing tensions relating to career choice, (b) expanding perceptions of career options, and (c) developing career exploration and planning skills.

Reflecting on the Data to Determine Next Steps

Following Cycle 1, as the authors reflect on the outcomes from the interviews, they recognize providing the training in career exploration also increases students' self-efficacy for career exploration and decision making, which is consistent with Bandura's (1986, 1997) theory on self-efficacy. Additionally, they acknowledge that triangulating these results in a new study by gathering data from an additional source, the Strategic Academic/Career Planning Project, will make the results more credible. As a result, the first author undertakes Cycle 2 in this AR project.

Taken together, results from the two cycles of AR show life science students are able to engage in the self-reflection, research, and analytical tasks that comprise the career development process. As job markets tend to shift and various occupations' availability and requirements tend to constrict, this study indicates college students need to be introduced to these career planning activities to improve their own self-efficacy, which will lead to more efficient and appropriate job search processes and the potential for increased job satisfaction.

Limitations

As with any research study, particularly an action research project, threats to validity must be considered and acknowledged. One primary threat, history, maintains events other than the treatment occur at the same time and influence the dependent variable (Smith & Glass, 1987). For example, students may become extraordinarily interested in career planning activities and they spend additional time and effort outside the scope of the study, which may influence their scores.

An additional threat to validity is the experimenter effect (Smith & Glass, 1987). It is possible that the researcher's "charm and energy" could "motivate their research subjects to perform particularly well" (p. 149). This is especially challenging in action research, where delivery of the intervention is carried out by the researcher/instructor. This is an issue because the first author teaches the course.

To build validity and trustworthiness of the interpretations of the qualitative data, we collected multiple data including interviews and course assignments (Mertler, 2017). To establish credibility of the interpretations of the data, the first author engaged in a systematic process of coding and interpreting the qualitative data. She completed two cycles of coding using Strauss and Corbin's (1998) and Saldaña's (2016) techniques. Moreover, she employed multiple coding methods, careful reflection at each step of the process, analytic memos to guide her efforts, and systematic processes to ensure the data supported the interpretations.

Implications for Practice

Upon the conclusion of the dissertation, it is natural to think "Where do we go from here?" Although considerable change can occur through the actions of one individual, we realize that the implications for this study actually are at a systemic level: (a) prioritizing career development in this institution; and (b) increasing dialogue about career development in the academic advising community.

Prioritizing Career Development in Higher Education

In the literature, there is a divide in higher education regarding the explicit prioritization of students' career development as compared to providing education for education's sake (Chan, 2016). Although ASU does not specifically indicate a stance with respect to career development in the mission or vision statements, many processes and organizational structures suggest a strong commitment of students' career development. Thus, a major implication is that higher education leaders should revisit their institution's views on and activities related to career preparation and development because more could be done on a systemic level to ensure consistency with respect to promotion and implementation of career development resources and education.

At ASU, career development courses are taught, but are not offered in a major/discipline-specific format. Results from a survey, conducted prior to Cycle 1, indicate 87% of SOLS' alumni support a discipline-specific course. Further, this feedback is also prevalent in the interviews from the dissertation. All of this points to the recommendation that career development activities are appreciated by students when offered in a tailored format. Thus, higher education leaders should move away from large, catch-all career development activities and provide resources and support for academic units to offer career development activities for their own student populations through deliberate immersion using career development materials in the curriculum and programming.

Increasing Dialogue About Career Development in the Academic Advising Community

Frequently, "students' career development" is a polarizing topic among academic advisors. Either advisors relish the opportunity to discuss career planning activities or heavily doubt their capacity to facilitate this conversation. The latter group of advisors would rather introduce the students to the career advising resources on campus and avoid this more complex conversation altogether. There are a variety of possible solutions for this aversion to career advising.

First, there is a need to hold conversations about counseling skills. Some institutions require academic advisors to be formally trained in counseling, whereas others, do not. This intervention and study are rooted in career psychology, so one implication could be to require academic advisors to learn about advising related to career advising/counseling.

Second, another way to mitigate this matter is to revisit the organizational structure of academic and career advising. Some institutions actually merge their career and academic advising units into one advising department, instead of having them separated. ASU's philosophy is that academic and career advising are separate entities. Thus, there is an opportunity for discussions about the roles of academic and career advisors, as well as providing resources on how the two types of advisors' efforts overlap and can support one another.

CONCLUSION

As an advisor, the first author often shares with others that "students don't know what they don't know" about career possibilities and the career planning process.

Nevertheless, through courses such as the one offered in these studies, students develop career exploration and planning skills, resulting in increased knowledge, skills, and self-efficacy with respect to career exploration. Ultimately, this study reveals that career development programming is needed for and appreciated by college students, affording many opportunities for academic units and the university to reconsider their prioritization of career development activities. Finally, if institutions are committed to the notion that "A baccalaureate education should prepare students for a particular profession or advanced study and for constructive and satisfying personal, social and civic lives as well," (ASU Academic catalog: University undergraduate general studies requirement, 2020) then more needs to be done in academic discipline areas to make these laudable goals a reality.

REFERENCES

Arizona State University. (2020). *Academic catalog: University undergraduate general studies requirement.* https://catalog.asu.edu/ug_gsr

Bandura, A. (1986). *Social foundations of thought and action: A social-cognitive theory.* Prentice-Hall.

Bandura, A. (1997). *Self-efficacy: The exercise of control.* W. H. Freeman and Company.

Chan, R. Y. (2016). Understanding the purpose of higher education: An analysis of the economic and social benefits for completing a college degree. *Journal of Education Policy, Planning and Administration, 6*(5), 1–40. https://scholar.harvard.edu/roychan/publications/understanding-purpose-higher-education-analysis-economic-and-social-benefits

Fayer, S., Lacey, A., & Watson, A. (2017, January 13). *STEM occupations: Past, present, and future.* U.S. Bureau of Labor Statistics. https://www.bls.gov/spotlight/2017/science-technology-engineering-and-mathematics-stem-occupations-past-present-and-future/home.htm

Guba, E. G. (1981). Criteria for assessing the trustworthiness of naturalistic inquiries. *Educational Communication and Technology, 29*(2), 75–91.

Holland, J. L. (1985). *Making vocational choices: A theory of vocational personalities and work environments* (2nd ed.). Prentice-Hall.

Holland, J. L. (1997). *Making vocational choices: A theory of vocational personalities and work environments* (3rd ed.). Prentice-Hall.

Kennelly, E., Sargent, A., & Reardon, R. (2018, February 13). *RIASEC literature from 1953–2016: Bibliographic references to Holland's theory, research, and applications* (technical report no. 58). The Center for the Study of Technology in Counseling and Career Development, Florida State University. https://career.fsu.edu/sites/g/files/upcbnu746/files/TR-%2058.pdf

Mertler, C. A. (2017). *Action research: Improving schools and empowering educators* (5th ed.). Sage Publications, Inc.

Noonan, R. (2017, March 30). *STEM jobs: 2017 update.* Office of the Chief Economist, Economics and Statistics Administration, United States Department of Commerce. https://www.commerce.gov/sites/default/files/migrated/reports/stem-jobs-2017-update.pdf

Peterson, G. W., Sampson, J. P., Jr., Reardon, R. C., & Lenz, J. G. (2003). *Core concepts of a cognitive information processing approach to career development and services.* The Career Center, Florida State University. https://career.fsu.edu/sites/g/files/imported/storage/original/application/1ace86a5725b4cc0e16ddcb14c9d2930.pdf

Reardon, R. C., & Lenz, J. G. (2015). *Handbook for using the self-direction search: Integrating RIASEC and CIP theories in practice.* PAR, Inc.

Reardon, R. C., Lenz, J. G., Peterson, G. W., & Sampson, J. P. (2019). *Career development & planning: A comprehensive approach. Student edition* (6th ed.). Kendall Hunt Publishing Company.

Saldaña, J. (2016). *The coding manual for qualitative researchers* (3rd ed.). Sage Publications, Inc.

Sampson, J. P., Jr., Osborn, D. S., Bullock-Yowell, E., Lenz, J. G., Peterson, G. W., Reardon, R. C., Dozier, V. C., Leierer, S. J., Hayden, S. C. W., & Saunders, D. E. (2020). *An introduction to CIP theory, research, and practice.* (Technical Report No. 62). Center for the Study of Technology in Counseling & Career Development, Florida State University. https://purl.lib.fsu.edu/diginole/FSU_libsubv1_scholarship_submission_1593091156_c171f50a

Sampson, J. P., Jr., Reardon, R. C., Peterson, G. W., & Lenz, J. L. (2004). *Career counseling and services: A cognitive information processing approach.* Center for the Study of Technology and Career Development. Florida State University. https://career.fsu.edu/sites/g/files/upcbnu746/files/files/tech-center/ncda-presentations/2011/201107_408CIP_PPT.pdf

Smith, M. L., & Glass, G. V. (1987). *Research and evaluation in education and the social sciences.* Allyn & Bacon.

Strauss, A., & Corbin, J. (1998). *Basics of qualitative research: Techniques and procedures for developing grounded theory* (2nd ed.). Sage Publications Inc.

BIOGRAPHIES

EDITORS

Sara B. Ewell is the Associate Dean of Faculty Affairs for the College of Professional Studies and Teaching Professor in the Graduate School of Education at Northeastern University. She previously served as the Assistant Dean of the Graduate School of Education and Director of the Doctor of Education which was awarded the Carnegie Project of the Education Doctorate 2022 Program of the Year Award under her leadership. Dr. Ewell's research interests include social justice, educational leadership, urban education, teacher preparation and retention, and qualitative research. Previously, Dr. Ewell taught at the University of North Carolina, Stonehill College and as K–12 classroom teacher.

Joan Giblin is an Associate Teaching Professor in the Graduate School of Education at Northeastern University. She serves as the Dissertation Lead for the EdD program and as served as faculty lead for the M.Ed. in Higher Education Administration program. Prior to Northeastern, Dr. Giblin held leadership roles in residence life, orientation programs, first year seminar, academic support programs and academic advising as well as provided strategic leadership for student support and retention initiatives. Her research interests include academic self-regulation,

---

Faculty Development: Achieving Change Through Action Research, pages 127–131.
Copyright © 2024 by Information Age Publishing
www.infoagepub.com
All rights of reproduction in any form reserved.

intentional instructional design, and the field of higher education. In addition to teaching in both the doctorate and masters' programs, she also serves as an elected official on her local school board.

Joe McNabb is a full-time faculty member in the Graduate School of Education. Prior to joining the faculty, he completed an 11-year term as president of Labouré College. This position followed a 17-year tenure as professor and dean of faculty. He served as a commissioner, a six-year term, on the New England Commission of Higher Education (NECHE). He also chaired, or served as a site visitor, for many accreditation teams throughout the United States and several in Europe. He has also served on many boards, including teaching hospitals, community educational agencies, and several non-profit organizations.

AUTHOR BIOGRAPHIES

Kathryn Bell, EdD, serves as the Director of the School of Healthcare Administration and Leadership, and Director and Professor in the Doctor of Science Program, at Pacific University in Hillsboro, Oregon. Kathryn joined Pacific University in 2010 as a full-time faculty member in the School of Dental Hygiene Studies. She served as the Associate Dean for Interprofessional Education from 2018-2023 and was appointed as the founding director of the Doctor of Science Program in 2021. Her research interests include issues facing graduate education and interprofessional education. She currently serves on the Interprofessional Committee for the Association of Schools Advancing Health Professions (ASAHP) and is a member of the American Dental Education Association (ADEA) and American Dental Hygienists' Association (ADHA).

Nicole Brewer, EdD, is the Director of the Academic Coaching Center and an assistant professor of humanities at Anna Maria College in Paxton, Massachusetts. Her research focuses on reforming developmental education and academic support methods in higher education, and she has a specific interest in improving the college experience for historically underrepresented students. She is a contributor and a co-editor of *UDL University: Designing for Variability across the Postsecondary Curriculum*, which is a multi-contributor volume of narratives about implementing UDL in higher education. She also co-authored a book with her father titled *Withstanding the Lie*, which helps people cope with the mental and emotional harm caused by bigotry.

Ray Buss, PhD, is professor of educational psychology and educational research in the Mary Lou Fulton Teachers College at Arizona State University. He teaches research and methodology courses and supervises doctoral students in the college's highly recognized EdD program in the division of educational leadership and innovation. His research focuses on doctoral students' development of identities as educational leaders and educational researchers; examines instructional issues and outcomes in the doctoral program including graduates' use of inquiry skills; and explores infusion of technology into the college's teacher preparation courses and its effects on technology integration by teacher candidates as they work toward conducting instruction in their classrooms. From 1992-2007, he served as graduate studies coordinator, graduate director, and assistant dean of the college.

Serena Christianson, EdD, recognized for her exceptional achievements as an academic success advising coordinator at Arizona State University's (ASU) School of Life Sciences, is the Learning Communications and Operations Program Manager for the Sales, Marketing, and Communications Group at Intel Corporation. She has been honored by the National Academic Advising Association (NACADA) for her outstanding contributions, making her the fifth advisor from ASU to receive this recognition. She brings to her role a wealth of experience, including an MBA with an emphasis in leadership and significant contributions to career development courses.

Jacob Cragg, EdD, serves as the Director of Learning Design and Technology for Northeastern University's D'Amore-McKim School of Business. Additionally, he serves as a part-time faculty for Northeastern University's Graduate School of Education within the College of Professional Studies. He specializes in digital content and assessment creation, learning analytics, micro credentials, as well as faculty and staff development emphasizing learning design and technology. Prior to joining Northeastern in 2018, Cragg served as a secondary educator, coach, and technology coordinator in his home state of Arkansas.

Jodie Donner, EdD, is an award-winning learning experience developer and educator currently working as a Senior Instructional Designer at Committee for Children. Jodie has more than 20 years' experience in the educational technology field, during which time she has helped build Second Step® SEL for Adults and a high school social-emotional learning program currently being field tested, co-created a technology course for preservice teachers, and co-designed and led professional learning aimed at the equitable advancement of computer science education for underserved students. Building professional learning communities is a prominent focus of her work, presentations, and publications.

Eric Hofmann, Ed.D., is Associate Dean for Academic Affairs at LaGuardia Community College (City University of New York), where he has oversight of learning assessment, first-year and capstone academic and co-curricular programs, and peer mentoring. He also serves as the PI on several federally-funded student success projects. Eric has written about college transition strategies and ePortfolio practice and was co-editor of the New Direction in Higher Education volume, *Dual Enrollment: Strategies, Outcomes, and Lessons for School—College Partnerships* (2012).

Melanie Kasparian, MBA, serves as the Director of Assessment and Planning within Student Affairs and Inclusive Excellence at the University of Denver. Previously, she worked at Northeastern University in Instructional Design, Faculty Development, and Assessment. She partners with faculty fellows and student affairs leadership to bridge the gap between curricular and co-curricular spaces to assess the student experience. She is passionate about harnessing the power of data and the potential of artificial intelligence to shape educational experiences for all learners.

Björg LeSueur, MEd, serves as program coordinator and clinical associate professor for the early childhood studies program in the division of educational leadership and innovation at the Mary Lou Fulton Teachers College. Björg boasts over two decades of experience in the early childhood education field, with a focus on early childhood special education, inclusion, collaborative practice, teacher-child interactions, and instructional impact on child outcomes. Björg is committed to supporting and empowering early childhood educators, by engaging in innovative leadership that fosters the professional journeys of those that serve our youngest learners.

Tanya Pinkerton, MEd, serves as a clinical assistant professor in the division of teacher preparation for Mary Lou Fulton Teachers College. Prior to joining Arizona State University, Ms. Pinkerton spent ten years teaching preschool and elementary-aged children in a publicschool setting with a focus on educating students with disabilities in an inclusive school environment. Ms. Pinkerton is committed to on-going engagement in teacher preparation spaces, especially those that serve future special education teachers.

Kathleen Puckett, Ph.D., is an associate professor in the Mary Lou Fulton Teachers College at Arizona State University. Her areas of interest include inclusive practices for students with disabilities and instructional and assistive technology. She is the 2023 president of the Division of Leaders and Legacy, and past president of the Council for Exceptional Children (2009).

Mamta Saxena, PhD, is the Assistant Dean of Academic Quality and Assessment at Northeastern University, College of Professional Studies, and has taught as part-time faculty in the Graduate School of Education. Before joining Northeastern, she led the instructional design team at Southern New Hampshire University for their online programs and has worked in corporate and academic settings both in India and in the United States. She has published on the topics of globalized e-learning, assessment, and equity. She serves as the Vice President of the New England Education Assessment Network (NEean); an evaluation team member at the New England Commission of Higher Education (NECHE); and on the DEI committee at the Association for the Assessment of Learning in Higher Education (AALHE).

Andrea Weinberg, PhD, is an esteemed expert in the field of teacher education, with a particular emphasis on preparing educators to navigate the challenges of a climate-affected world. Through innovative training programs and curricula, she equips teachers with the tools to deliver culturally sensitive, socially just, and environmentally conscious education. She is current an Associate Professor at Arizona State University.